After Mother

Barbara Heaton Latham

First published in Great Britain in 2017 by

BookBorn Publications

Email: info@bookborn.co.uk

Cover by Mike Harding from a photo by Clare Murphy

ISBN-13: 978-0-9957008-0-2
ISBN-10: 099570080X

www.barbaralatham.co.uk

ACKNOWLEDGMENTS

I would like to thank all those with whom I have found engaging conversations, above all John Heaton, and thank those who have read this and offered comments.
For the work to make this text available thanks to Fatima Raja, Debbie Cass and William Shone. And for the synopsis thanks to Jude Heaton.

INTRODUCTION

Through the 1950's, life in small town New Zealand was seemingly solid though we were there because the severe financial depression marked our father and the grim distant war left photographs of absent men, while others returned harmed.

Yet we children were to be a bright future, with education and respectability the keys. Happy families was the game in play and ours, apparently, particularly reliable.

That was until May 1966.

Events that followed were written of in different forms.

A pile of notes on scraps of paper ended up in a folder with my mother's name on it.

Those are now all in the first person addressing her as "you."

Some of a narrative account, written 20 years ago, has been juxtaposed with the notes.

ZERO STAR BRANDY

The tears' words get completely lost.
When disorder speaks, order must keep silent
- loss has great experience.
Now we must stand by
pointlessness.
So, that memory gradually may regain its eloquence
and give good counsel on longevity
to all that has died.

Let's stand by this little
photograph
that's still in the bloom of its future:
young people somewhat pointlessly embracing one
another
in front of an anonymously cheerful beach.
Nauplion Euboea Skopelos?
You'll say
where wasn't there sea back then.

Kiki Dimoula

A

I am like Montaigne "unsuited to continuous
discourse."

Joubert

i.

I began to keep a folder for you.
What else was there to do with all the scraps of things
which couldn't now be said direct?
At least a heap of notes are in your name.
I never tried to write soon after your death. The worst
faded but tipped up confidence in what it was I knew.

*

Before you died I'd accumulated words, not realising
how little some were understood.

"Dead" and "mother" put together tightened up the chest. I used them first only as a challenge: "No, she won't recover, she will die."

It came out to shock. But then could not be swallowed back.

I'd said what would now have to be lived.

ii.

From a distance of years, phone calls stand as pegs to tie in something of what has receded.

A hostel warden who took the first said you were in a distant hospital, not catching the ferry to come up to me as expected.

Was I warned not to hurry to you, or did that thought not occur? How would I get down to Christchurch? Where could I stay? Travelling was not yet on my horizon.

A light telegram was sent instead, before I realised there were head injuries as well as the crushed pelvis.

I was supposed to be dancing with a graduating cousin but went instead to make a call in the student hostel phone booth. Whom I sought to contact is long forgotten but not the jamming door. I rang the exchange, having used up my cash and it being free but, as it was graduation and a week of student stunts, I was not believed.

I stayed locked in a place for conversation with no chance of making contact.

It was my brother who eventually came, forcing that red door, having driven down 200 miles from our town, to Wellington, to get me.

Early next morning he drove fast, getting us home in record time and rushing in to a phone already ringing.

4

The news from the hospital was that the attempt to relieve pressure in your skull only confirmed you would die.

While we waited the rest of an unreal day, my brother kept busy making phone calls to relations and friends, then sent me out with the dog.

He took the dawn call and didn't need to speak, that first loud ring told what couldn't yet be digested.

iii.

Sentences started forming after I gave birth, nearly ten years later.

Forgetful of permanent absence I lay in a hormone haze of expectation that you must come.

When a doctor called for me, he called out your name, and for that moment I thought you had arrived.

He looked astonished by my fight and tears: "Mrs" was your title and not mine, so would he be more careful!

But once I became a mother too, our connection came alive.

These notes began and while writing I felt less lonely.

iv.

In the period after your car crash the air grew thick with euphemism, as if no-one fully believed you who'd been alive were only ashes.

At least it made us laugh that only one said "dead" in their card, and that was Bunyan's death.

They called you "remarkable" or "the most alive" as your death briefly elevated you, and us.
Mail came in bagfuls.

Until that accident I took your solidity for granted. Perhaps your crushed bones scared others too, a reminder of destroying forces, as we began stepping less securely.

v.

Although this centres on events decades ago, I usually prefer to tell that which others cannot denounce as inaccurate, it being only "a story".

Something of what happened then is sure. Newspapers record the fact and all agree to a date of death on a gravestone. But to believe someone once alive can be dead and not abandon them, or hold to them as if they are still living, is an act of faith. At that time I was not up to it. "Everyone dies one day," I could say easily, but that "one day" put death off. Mother wasn't a pet or a grandparent. I knew those died on you. That someone still part of me was suddenly dead required considerable adjustment in a teenager geared to expanding life.

I came near to believing something unspeakable when I went to the airport to collect a young Japanese woman, who had been waiting for mother on a Christchurch street corner. I still do not know how she came to hear of the accident. How long did she wait in public in a strange city, for the car that would never come? She was in her early twenties, learning English at mother's side and filling a place daughters were vacating, she, too, had gone visiting down south. (After the crash, her attachment being insufficient to keep her near the bedside, the Japanese woman was put on a plane to join me, where I'd just begun my first term at university.) Mother had been due to come to me but postponed. It was during her one day of delay that she smashed a borrowed car. I was informed her pelvis was crushed but she'd been able to sing to a frightened child with her in the ambulance.

"Six weeks," the medical director told father, before she could be moved up north for local nursing. Hours later, he added "Come quickly!"

When father left home by car for the considerable journey south he probably did not believe there was serious danger, the doctors not confirming that head injury till it was too late to fly. But there must have been the possibility of brain damage. I now know there always is after such a fall. Perhaps father believed the optimistic version he told his children. Maybe, however pressing his need, he could never push a claim; if the airline said no seats were available he would not even state his case. He drove alone, asking politely at two airports en route, and did not arrive while she was conscious.

Even the first account of the accident threw me, mother was usually the one in control. I knew none of the detail, I did not know she was flung from a car that had itself been tossed up in the air but it seemed an outrageous flipping of order. (When I was eight, to avoid children straggling across the road in rain, she had to swerve and hit their dog. After watching her fail to manage everything, I had to be sent home from school as ill.)

As I stood on the tarmac waiting, I could only wonder if I was "creating" again. I expected the Japanese woman to tease, or once more call me "too intense," but as she came down off the plane this young woman caught my eye and did an about turn. She could not face me! If she turned from me there must be no hope to press in a hug. Or maybe it was her limited English, she might have misunderstood – "Mamma looks very bad. You do not see it is Mamma. Yesterday they would not let me go in – today they will be cutting open Mamma's head." I had called Joan by her Christian name for many years, this older Japanese girl called her "Mamma."

*

That evening two cousins would graduate from university. Like father, one had become a surprisingly good sportsman and gently protective of the women in his life. I relied on his kindness. The other cousin was headstrong and vital, her life sparkled. My colouring was nearer hers than any of my sisters.

The day went on and on. I can still see the tattered phone book, a wad of it loose from the binding, in the telephone booth from which I had to be rescued. There was overwhelming unreality in everything yet also precise detail. I can hear the conversation at dinner where I sat with celebrating aunts who believed mother would recover from a broken hip and soon be up; hers was a shockingly strong constitution, aunts being more "delicate". On father's side, these women inclined to "temperament," while mother's female relatives seemed formidably designed to hold their world in place and celebrate it. I had no doubt where I'd got any of my inconvenient ways.

"Your mother will take things in her stride, she is marvellous."

My "No, she is having brain surgery," stopped conversation. I was excused the rest of the party and as I crept off one cousin was tender, the other spread her warmth. I remember a thought "if this does happen, will I ever be happy the way she is tonight, in love with a Maori man, full of it and at the centre of her family?"

*

My big brother, arriving to pick up the petite Japanese woman and myself, said I was being dramatic. I hoped so, but then why cut open her head? Confronted by phone with the fact that we knew of the surgery, father conceded it was worse and they'd know by next morning. So we drove over two hundred miles home in a borrowed Citroen. The phone was ringing as we pulled up and my brother having rushed ahead was saying, "So what do we tell the girls?" "The truth," I said, without thinking if I really wanted to know, and he had no time to come up with anything else. "It's hopeless, surgery was no use, she'll die today."

The Japanese woman was despatched again and all there was to do was wait. By late afternoon my brother was pacing up and down the long hall of our colonial home. He liked to organise, but you can't manage death and he'd finished ringing relations.

"Go for a walk," he said. And so I took the dog, not on my usual route quickly away from town, but along its wide streets as if heading to the one secondary school, where I'd biked for years.

*

"Come in, come in. We're having tea in a moment," invited a father concerned for my mother, struck down where none of them could visit. "Still, we'll soon have her in the local hospital," his wife said.
"No, she is going to die!"
The shock was sharp. I'd said it now! Why had I been unable to resist startling them, when they thought they knew, as adults always did? I knew only that my mother would not be transferred for them to visit. The rest was an abyss.
I was quickly sent off but invited back later, after the hostess's five children were dispatched to the pictures. Whatever was happening it was setting me apart from old school companions; if I was bringing in a dying mother, they would be treated to the movies.

vi.

When last we met, we kissed, waved goodbye and separated.
Your final departure left torn edges.
Later I tried to blame the fact that your broken flesh was kept from sight and I could hardly find my farewell in that crowded funeral, where the concern was with not being felled, not letting father down, not pulling him back to that too brief shared collapse on the floor. Decent behaviour was expected, he said, and we must all stand it.

*

The packed church needed speakers outside for the overflow.
Flowers covered the floor of the hall.
Some response was shared in the press of embrace, despite my daze, but then began the long living with absence.

*

That you were gone became real – an empty place headed our long table where you'd reigned.
Someone else had to decide what to buy, once people stopped bringing cakes to add to tins piled high.

Your close friend stayed faithful, leaving father's favourite date scones at the door.
Obviously you were not coming back but could just be in hiding, having had enough of us and small town life. Maybe, like me, you were ready for something bigger.
Not much made sense.

vii.

For a brief moment others dropped their lives to offer concern.
But how could another meet my hurt, when I barely knew what it was, let alone how to show it?

*

Though we had always been acceptable before, our family now presented something awkward.

All kinds of people felt up to you now, even if they were also discomposed, and women, who'd never dared take liberties while you were alive, felt free to walk right into your kitchen.

But for those others your drama was soon over, whereas the coffin went from sight far ahead of our stunned cells adjusting.

*

There was little spare capacity to attend to otherwise interesting new subjects.

Though when I spoke of you it sounded like an obituary on repeat. I bored even myself.

It wasn't that new sadness was added to us. We belonged in a different club now. We lost step with embarrassed friends. They weren't absorbed by death – for them teenage sex came first and dying could wait its turn to take up importance.

*

Having felt ready to leave the enclosure of home, the promising "out there" of cinema and city no longer drew me.

The magnetism of friends pulled less and any appetite to party shrivelled.

As far back as I knew there was playing on my own and being with others, but this being out of phase felt cold.

I didn't fit back with those for whom your accident was in the past.
The rupture left me jumpy – phone calls setting off a "who now?" anxiety.
The seemingly solid having cracked, everyone became precarious, everything unstable.

*

Having been clothed in adolescent bright shades of immortality, having strode in over expectant hopes of increasing mastery, there could no longer be that straight path. A vast gap had opened up by the shockingly arbitrary.

Then I began to come across disasters.
They must have happened before but barely impinged; I had not walked into them, they went on elsewhere.
Now they were what had to be stomached.
Or was I to become the town crier, calling out a warning I couldn't quite accept, that the terrible really does happen?

viii.

If you had known walking to that ferry would be your final glimpse of me, how might it have been?
What if I'd understood, then, and known it was the end to being your daughter?

13

I should be grateful, after all, it oozed intermittently into me, yet I also wish I'd asked for your farewell to being my mother. Instead, with friends, I cheered at your ferry's departure for the south, where I'd never been.

When you had called in on your way to Christchurch, I didn't admit to having been homesick those first few weeks away from home. But did gear myself to insist that, unlike my sisters, I was not prepared to be a debutante.

When you simply agreed it was astonishing!

Then we spent our last afternoon together buying beautiful and bright silk, instead of debutante white, for an alternative ball gown.

ix.

You were the centre of family life and when you dropped we scattered apart.

Left to watch his loss, unable to make it right, we tried to carry on for him as if, perhaps, it hadn't also happened to us.

(And maybe he was doing something of the same.)

We had been "family" but your death emphasised how far we each had differing and unfinished ties to you.

* *

I went for an eye test, puzzled by not being able to read as I did before your death.

The optician was adamant – he wouldn't consider glasses "for at least a year after trauma."

"These things take time to settle," he said, and I skipped home. At last feeling lighter!

He had taken seriously that something had happened to me, as well as you.

But his even greater gift was promising that I might see straight in a year.

x.

Decades on it is still possible to gag on the fact that you are never coming back – that you who were in my existence could just leave with no goodbye.

There was nothing to be done to keep you. It was all over and not a single thing could make it different!

That was the crushing defeat and how I laboured to forgive it.

Through those years of barely acknowledged frustration, focus was on the way it was handled. I couldn't quite accept that all of us were powerless.

And there was indignation - if you were gracious to ambulance men, why not send a message home?

If you sang to the scared girl who was also in the ambulance, why not reach out to your daughters?

I failed to see you as entirely subject. The power of life and death, like fairies, were outgrown – till you showed me – dying to do it!

When death came for you I had no importance, even if this took an age to recognise.

I became just a distant audience, though I had been part of you and fighting free.

Once you were the source of life and needed. As we grew, you seemed pushed from centre to side, but your death proved you had still been the ground beneath my feet.

As long as I remember my mother was happy to be thought younger than she was. That she was younger than father was freely admitted but not her age. Her gravestone gives only her date of death. When she died I preferred her younger than she was. If she was forty-nine as we and her best friends calculated, or worse maybe fifty-one, having denied she had reached fifty, that was terribly old, nearly old enough to be finished with living. Her black hair already grey. It did feel alarming for her to be snatched so abruptly but thirty was old to me and one had to be young for death to be in the least bit tragic. Following much the same logic I wanted to be younger than I was.

At eighteen who needs a mother? I had, after all, until recently been spending hours in limbo from the town and family, walking and running out into the country with the dog. Only six weeks before, I had left home altogether, hiding homesickness inside pining for that energetic dog. I had, of course, taken for granted when I left that home would stay standing behind me. I had also taken as inevitable that, despite her litany of "I told you so, now you see what I meant," mother would stay to take care of the mongrel during term time.

But without mother's control the dog would be entirely unruly at her funeral and visitors in best black would be leapt upon with muddy paws. I had delighted in his outrageous ways, it was she who subdued him to discipline. Eventually the death, which brought the dog's banishment, gave me more direct access to my father. At first I could not imagine him without her, his place in the family seemed to be through her. I still believed she was the stronger. I also feared the unbearable if I had to watch him. I'd often take on his worry, whether willing slow cars off the road if we were late to visit his mother, or pinching sisters under the table to keep hidden fights that upset him. With mother you kept out of sight what would incur her wrath but with father it was a graver matter of keeping from him jealousy, rage and all unpleasantness really. Surely we couldn't keep a dead mother out of sight? But we did try.

xii.

While waiting for your death I told a woman you would not survive and added that I hoped his plane crashed before he got home.
Perhaps my startling plea came from imagining that he could not cope without you.
Managing with no parents seemed a possibility (the previous time you were both away we painted the bathroom lurid colours) but the prospect of having to watch him suffer seemed beyond me.
Little did I know how soon I'd be repeating "I have my father back", as if you'd claimed him over my cooling years, then failed to take him with you.

Casting off teenage withdrawal, I fled back and flung arms wide to embrace him. Afraid he, too, might take my separation seriously and simply vanish.
With him I would keep tight hold and felt a flood of gratitude for his survival.
I began to live in dread his death might finish me completely.

*

It started rolling off my tongue that I "loved my
father." It had not entered my head to say it before.
Declaring love was not, then, a convention, but when
I flung off a telegram from university to his work to
tell I loved him his staff were much amused.

Whether or not I assumed you loved me, I couldn't
say.

Tuning in to you was not what I'd routinely done, it
was his moods I sensed and tried to accommodate.

I barely asked how it might be for you to have your
life cut off, though having had you central in my life,
it seemed inconceivable to be nothing to you.

*

I turned again to him. He'd hoped for gentleness and
peace at home, with horrors kept outside the door
and battles for the sports field.

But ease in family life doesn't outlast a mother
smashed.

In the months after the funeral his footfall became a
rhythm for sleep. Up and down the corridor his hard
nights were walked.

High wood ceilings absorbed his restless need not to
be seen at a loss.

He didn't like my being a witness.

xiii.

The night mother was dying, I went to my sister's
room, and when she returned from a school reunion

ball tried to climb into her bed. She, assuming mother cheerful, if in plaster, pushed me away and wanted sleep. When the phone rang, very early, I knew; my sister could only shout for quiet. When I say "I knew" what the phone call was, that is language running ahead of itself. I knew it was father to say our mother was dead. We were spared detail; holiday plans or weddings were matters to be discussed with daughters. The accident was not explained, nor the whereabouts of our car if father drove down and flew back. The memorial at the school was just there one day, to surprise my younger sister. Little wonder I thought detail was what you had to make up to fit the feel of whatever was going on.

The matter we were asked about was the rose for her grave after the ashes and stone were in place. "Peace", we agreed, a favourite in her own rose garden. Years later I went to see the grave in a very straight row of orderly stones, so removed from those across the world in England's old churchyards where I often wandered to read inscriptions and where some had four children in a grave. On those English stones I could not lay my bouquet and, finally, I went with a sister and flowers to mother's stone. Her rose was in bloom. It was a pink I'd always disliked. She'd said I should never wear that brash pink, not with my hair. It was not the pale lemon blushed with the subtle pink of "peace". I have no idea of its name nor of how it came to be there. I brought a decidedly pink shirt to match it and thought it suited me. Father, we had to accept, would never have insisted we got the rose we asked for, that was not how he lived; mother made the fuss. In any shop she got the best and demanded it, flirting as she shopped.

There was no-one now to fight the world for roses or for us.

xiv.

You left with no kiss or word.
Had you realised you were to die before you could see your children as adults, would that have made you weep?
I can't know. But that is one of my sorrows.
For you it might have been sheer attachment to living – not feeling ready to be plucked, as far as we know, for you planned a trip to Japan and New Mexico.

We heard only that the ambulance men were charmed – not who called them, or how long you waited on the road.
We heard you sang to your school friend's daughter despite pain, and could summon the hospital director, giving hope you might recover, until massive brain haemorrhage showed.

*

The facts took years to piece together. However, it was not so much the lack of coherent account that bothered, it was more the lack of conviction. When I went into our small town, having been shut inside for days, the impact was immediate. It simply could not be true! How could she be dead if the town was exactly as always, in shadow and sun up and down the High Street with shoppers in Woolworth's across from the bank? But disbelief rarely surfaced with such clarity, it smouldered beneath heaviness. Maybe she went back where she came from and couldn't bring herself to return for us to carry on leaving her? If she was finished with family life, to crash out was not as wilful as slamming a door. Perhaps something had finally snapped? It seemed as easy to believe as that they had actually burned her.

I never saw her dead. It was a week before her damaged body, cut up further for post-mortem, was sent back north. Possibly it didn't bear scrutiny; one who saw her insisted we were lucky to miss it, it haunted her for years, although father declared she looked as beautiful as the day he married her, when she had been tall, dark and lovely. Maybe she did but this was surprising.

When he arrived back home, having flown for the first time, it was possible to think she must be dead. He took us in his arms, huddling to the floor to weep, until that door bell cut in cruelly soon. We were to get up – "people will come" – and they did. Father protected his daughters from a body going in an oven but he too had to be protected; we must not upset or disgrace him. She had been the ground of family life, her energy generated gatherings, Christmas and daily celebrations of living; it had been more conceivable that she could wipe us out, or suffocate the life in us, than that she could be extinguished.

xv.

Cakes piled up in our kitchen; a collection such as we had never seen: a five layered Dolly Varden, fruit cakes, sponges, Pavlova, apple pies and loaves; we ran out of cake tins the first day and cakes covered the dining table that seated twelve. Those who came to

21

us, even the dearest, came with biscuits and scones, with aprons or tea towels. The adults aimed to cope without tears in front of children. But how could she possibly be dead if not one of her friends was crying? If even her favourite sister, being useful, kept dry eyed? Alone we could laugh at every variety of euphemism in those daily condolences which poured in, as we replied to hundreds. It was a few our own age who made it almost believable; my school friend went blotched red all up her neck to bright cheeks and another girl coming towards us up the street suddenly hid her face in our hedge. Obviously it wasn't easy for them to acknowledge a dead mother; my sister went to her friend and I watched as they locked together squashing greenery. Mother's death seemed to take us off paths and into hedges; before the funeral, there was hiding in the church hedge. This was to be got through without screaming, though it was to be our first sight of her coffin. It was for any who wanted to attend and we discovered everyone had turned up. Since the large church was overflowing, as our car pulled in we saw men setting up a speaking system for those crowded outside. A woman of some sense, whose husband had recently died, said "I could take you home but if you don't go in I think you will regret it." We went in and only the Japanese woman made a noise that sounded half owl.

*

During and after the service three faces stayed fixed before my eyes, two were from either side of the choir, behind the coffin. The man was huge and shambling, a butcher, better able to shape up cuts of mutton than his own undisciplined flesh, but he sang for her. Another face had the usual short permed grey hair yet, from her, passion could flow in song. The third was in one of the packed rows near the back of the church. He stood out, defined in the blur. He was a boy I fancied and it seemed he was there for me in that long walk down the aisle.

We walked with a father who in public life drew as little attention to himself as possible; mother never minded being on display. It was his manhood at stake and, with no women to claim us, we stood alongside him, honorary men, though with no manly responsibilities, we were to go back to tea and cakes after lingering with flowers. In the hall near the front door, after talk of hospitals and operations, a relation showed where she'd had trouble with stitches up her throat. A baby in arms, five months old, hit the displayed protruding tender chin and that punching little fist was much appreciated. Later, beside our long table carved in one piece, I wished for his punch again; a woman spoke to me of coconut. I could have her recipe, it was fresh coconut made the difference. I'd managed never to bake a cake in my life, avoiding it even in compulsory cookery classes, did she think I was going to begin?

The men took the body to the nearest city an hour away for cremation, and there were stories of an impossible uncle nearly pushed from the car on that journey.

With the funeral over there was little mention of her. Back where I had just started at university, her death had little meaning for anyone else, while I expected wipe out. Death no longer lurked behind the cemetery wall but lay in waiting to bag me or those I loved at any moment. With the bottom dropped out of security, it was obvious anyone could fall. There was a whole new world to which I'd been an outsider but into which I now moved, to see a face through a windscreen, glass in the eye, a crash outside my hostel room, as I walked by. (It would take years before I grew impatient – could I ever settle for daily life without such dramas? Would it make sense to be content and calm? Then gradually I no longer seemed to come across disasters.)

xvi.

Mother not being in control of the house meant we could try tinned food. And then there was father, who had once been the one to climb over but in more recent years took responsibility for maintaining the family nest, while mother ruled inside it. By moving close I learnt surprising things when we went walking; he knew plenty of people who enjoyed wife swapping with keys thrown into a hat, but he'd never fancied it. It had never, ever, occurred to me he might! Quite a lot, I began to realise, had never occurred to me about this man. I liked it when he asked after siblings, but mother's shoes were several sizes too big for me.

*

When I fell on our icy mountain, a couple of months after her death, father was not spared. He watched. An older sister extended a hand as I lost balance, but no one could reach me, I knew. I saw her hand with the certainty that she would not touch me. The falling happened in slow motion as I stretched towards her, our fingers almost meeting. Once I'd tipped over backwards it was triple speed as I shot down. For nights father was again unable to sleep: I had failed him dreadfully.

There had been other falls. When mother left to go to her dying mother, taking only the baby, I fell on concrete steps to split above the lip. And after an earlier fall, at three or four, I recall being shaken hard in my stunned state by a furious mother. "How many times have I told you never to play with car doors!"

She had rushed back to where I'd dropped out onto the road.

Father, who was driving us home from the beach, could not bear to have it mentioned.

And once again, as I was half aware, this man was trying hard not to look, while at this stage I had little interest in seeing anything less than dreadful.

Mine might be a small fall on that mountain but she'd fallen right out of life.

I tried to get the hang of it, tried to believe it real.

*

We grew into expectation that if needed you'd be there.

I kept belief in that, despite pulling away from care. Of course you'd come if I fell.

When I did fall, slipping past those mountain rocks, after the hit of your accident, you were dead and the father, who once might have kissed a bandage and put it right, proved too distraught.

Hurt somehow stuck in a groove that neither of you were there when needed. And it was a slow stumble into recognising others aren't necessarily what one surmised.

Love came again for an ordinary man, less than the shined ideal of a child, but still I strove to show I could do without good care.

How quickly I set out to prove I could go alone, staying in remote places on my own, to reassure myself I could never be caught out and so disconcertingly left again.

*

There was further change: "I never thought I'd see you getting plump," that same boy from the funeral said. For months there had been a load on me, food didn't comfort, as some glibly said, but weighed me down. Meals at home had turned desultory, hostel food wasn't up to much and eating no longer a pleasure. I'd been unsatisfactorily skinny, never putting on weight while mother cooked well and lived, but I gathered flesh. With her alive I'd wriggled away but her death had got me and a mind which had been excited by ideas and possibilities, found few new thoughts could get through a sluggishness.

xvii.

You cut me off mid-sentence.

It was by sinking into sound that I became light and mobile, dancing out of fleshy thickness; dancing out of confusing misery.

Absorbed by music I came back to life, my body open and responsive to it, I simply moved.

*

Before your death there had already been query as to
what might be solid, despite all that was flow and
fluid in me.
But where containing skin, having been attached to
you in ways unseen, became sucked off my bones
that pull left vacancy into which it seemed I might
drop and drop.
(If structure holding me in place had been rendered
shaky, my back took on holding off a possible
collapse and it would take decades to identify that
tension.)

*

You showed that staying alive was not up to you,
though you had apparently ruled.
We were expanding to find how much could be over
to us, when your greater strength lay detonated.
And we were rendered uncertain and new calf
wobbly.

xviii.

Early December it was a friend's birthday and we'd
have the weekend party at our house, father being a
pushover. He was never one to put a stop to
anything, even if he stayed awake all night he'd
venture no more than "I do hope you'll all be
sensible." "You have to trust your children," he said
but worried if he owed it to other parents to
intervene.

In the midst of the party a phone call told of another accident. Seven months after her graduation, her Maori husband was killed and the red haired cousin with ready warmth was left with the possibility of permanent damage.

At the hospital father whispered "she does look like you, doesn't she?" I'd not seen anyone turned more unlike herself – a face in pieces held together with blood clots and thread. Was that as he saw me? He'd never gone along with the notion of a family likeness between this cousin and me, even in the colouring we both inherited, I was darker, called coppertop, not red.

I'd believed father didn't much like my freckles appearing at seven. Freckles might be all that was dark and unacceptable making its way to the surface, but had he seen me for the last ten years as he saw the hideously stitched face? Nothing made sense. Possibly he looked on her with love and saw her only as lovely as he has seen my mother; I was learning he had capacities not to see what was there before him. Even so his words went round and round. My eyes could only see damage. Then could see nothing, something pulled tighter and tighter, and I gave up. I had to, if I lifted my head or looked at light I vomited.

*

Migraine they said, but I had my own certainty: "Finally the darkness has got me!" The lurking black pit which opened up with mother's death had closed about me. I'd completely fallen in.

For father, who was drained and longed for a break, my collapse was a further strain. Not that he actually spoke of it until years later, when I could say he also failed to be there for me. No one could get looked after, not even the loyal dog. With her not there we proved not to be reliable owners after all and my brother arranged for his friend to take him. Trust was betrayed. "Don't ever, ever have a dog," I took to saying "they are too trusting." I did not intend to trust again and there would be no more dogs.

*

The morning the migraine lifted I looked at the trees. I was near enough to childhood to remember everyday things could be surprising but this was astonishment! Whilst gripped by darkness my eyes must have been polished to glistening. It was nine months after the issue of a death certificate and, getting up, I organised a trip, informed father of my intentions and took no notice of his reservations. Taking a grey rucksack I headed south.
It marked the end of leaden passivity and I never put weight on again.

* * *

B

"The things we believe are difficult to conceive of
because it is difficult to talk about them."

Joubert

i.

When I went to seek what might have happened, I
barely knew that family you visited, yet wrote to your
school friend and got on an overnight ferry from
Wellington to Christchurch.

Ten months after your death I went to look for
something of you and had no idea it might prove such
a detour.

As soon as I got off one boat, I was offered a day in a
smaller one. The picnic was ready, three young men
and a small girl wanted me to go, so I agreed, not
then realising the child could only be included if I
went because none of the men could swim.

After lunch a storm blew up, we capsized and floundering in wild surf I found more than I could say.

Only in retrospect that drawn out drama seems a necessary part of your dying.

ii.

Two decades later I wrote myself as "she", as a lump beneath a sheet, silent beneath spare covering.

For hours there seems to be no movement, then she emerges, wearing a passed down, worn thin, home-made nightgown.

That young woman is eighteen, neither tall nor fleshy, and she walks to the bathroom apparently oblivious of anyone she passes. The door is locked and water is heard running; later the figure reappears, drinks glasses of water in the shared and tiny kitchen before returning to stillness on the bed.

This bathing is repeated up to three times a day.

As others increasingly worried, she is watched in the bathroom, first through a keyhole and then a stool is placed for someone to look through the two inch gap above the door.

Water is going out the overflow. She is seen sinking into the full tub past her chin till her nose is on the water's edge. She lies calmly in the bath and after about an hour she again goes under her sheet in a room for students passing a year or two between home and elsewhere.

The student who has the other bed is not in residence. She has no reason to be. It isn't term time.

Once the figure is back under the sheet there is no face willing to engage; such amorphousness belongs more to jellyfish than students in a Christian hostel and the warden cannot approve.

Back when she was still speaking the girl had rung the hostel requesting to return early to the room she'd occupied in her first year; there'd been another accident, this time in a boat, she couldn't possibly go home, her father would not cope. She had tried going to a sister but had overwhelming conviction she needed retreat, to stay alone in what mattered. The warden, knowing of recent incidents in that family and seeing herself as counsellor to her charges, was not sorry she chose the hostel; they could talk, sort out matters over sherry. With term not started there'd be time for helping.

The young woman said on the phone "I need quiet, can I come to my room?" She thought she made a clear request. The warden said "I'll meet your plane," and "Come to sherry, six-ish, you'll feel more like talking after rest."

Leaving the warden at the door to student quarters, she went in expecting emptiness, not three foreign students plus one who'd returned early to use the library, all with much to ask of sharks and fishermen and the rescue.

They had an object of interest, she had no inclination to join that conversation, and so there was disjunction.

"If it had been any later the fisherman said it might have been impossible to find the others in the dark."

Events seemed to make sense to them, but she longed

to sink silently with the sea which had so nearly claimed her. Having no wish to surface into a newsy account she abandoned them to chat, for having got away from family concern she did not owe strangers explanation, or displays of coping.

Relieved not to speak and trivialise, she failed to anticipate her silence might provoke reaction.

However, she did speak when a doctor was sent in. The warden called in the university GP on the second morning.

"Why can't they leave me?" she asked him. He had a kindly face she'd seen once before for a sore throat and she hoped for his protection. Surely it was obvious she was waterlogged and needed time. He tut-tutted over her damaged chest. The warden had already informed him of the boat tipped up, in cold rough surf, and then her swim. She tried to find the thing to say that he might declare: "Best leave her to her healing baths and get on with your own lives." Instead he announced her condition to be shock and over-exposure, for which tranquilisers were the thing. She protested that pills would blur her, but he knew best.

He satisfied the warden with two prescriptions, cream for gashes on her chest and heavy tranquilising "to distance the lass from trauma." Meantime rest made sense; staying on the bed became acceptable and tablets were brought there, night and morning. If she could speak to the GP the silence was obviously wilful; talking definitely would be better, the warden told her. She failed to take this advice even though she appeared to take the medicine.

The tablets, spat out as soon as the warden left, collected under the bed: if chemical fug was added to the haze, she might never find her way.

* * *

There was the silence: and there is a history of speaking about it. Deep beneath the waves, which roughly beat against a sinking boat, there was such quiet. That silence deep within the sea remains. Yet there is talk of it these long years later and the tale written in the third person.

* * *

Lying, body suspended warm in water; stilled except for a faint gurgle, since even one breath sends drops through the overflow.

It is a return which sometimes hovers near what might be there to find. What had been absolute left so little. To sink fully finally awaits us all, meanwhile what value whispers of such surrender? Faint, or pulsing through all else we might listen to, murmurs haunt those who turn an ear: whispers of return to merge once more in that waiting ocean. But until inevitable completion there is the shore: from water to rocks, from sea to sand, from silence to speech, building sand shapes till the tide moves in. A big enough castle right up the beach could last till king tide when everything is washed again.

I went down to where you came from. You went back and died there.

Adults dealt with it; I had to see for myself. I stepped off the ferry to meet those with whom you stayed, a school friend with two grown sons and one small daughter. We agreed to go out to sea to try a new boat; not the parents, but a further young man along with the child and me, making five of us in all.

It was at sea that you were found. On shore I heard some details of your delay for that one day.

I heard in Christchurch you'd stayed for a "night on the town". Father's version had been that since you couldn't get up to the funeral of an aged aunt, you stayed to mark her day of burial with your difficult sister, whom I'd never met. But your friend told how the two of you went out alone to celebrate your inheritance. You drank to planning travels. Your Japanese charge was taken off your hands and you were free to "let your hair down in style"; your expression. Your school friend didn't give details, only said how happy you were at having money that offered independence and you wondered where else to go after Japan and visiting your sister-in-law in New Mexico.

Next day you had only to collect the Japanese girl, whom your friend's married daughter left at a corner park less than two miles away. Her English wasn't good, you didn't like to leave her waiting, so when the promised car did not come back you asked the aged grandmother about the old car in the shed. You found the car keys and had no way of knowing the clutch needed fixing. The small girl wanted to come with you, not stay with her grandmother; I don't know why she wasn't at school, she was seven years old, but perhaps it was still too early. The rest of the family had left for work, except one son who had the car he should have returned. You drove to the main road; everyone agreed you were quite stationary at a "give way". A car was speeding in a 30mph zone, judging from pedestrians, the degree of impact and from his driving history, still he had the gall to sue your estate. As he passed you were unmoving. The pair of you made eye contact, he said. It was in getting ready to go that you put the car in gear. It bunny hopped and caught the tail end of his Jaguar; your tinny car was flung into the air and you were thrown out on the road. People on foot saw it, but there was only one other car on the empty road and that driver didn't come forward; the Jaguar sped past him half a block back and he was wanted as a speed witness. Father paid off the Jaguar owner, you were dead and he couldn't deal with a case where you might be blamed. The police were insistent he should not, it was obvious the other party had been driving far too fast, let it come to court, but father wanted it settled. I heard this in the water from the young man who had been driving home late, knowing you wanted the car; it was him the Jaguar passed. This was the same young man who thought I should take the only life jacket and save myself; he wanted no further blame on his family. I liked him and we briefly considered losing virginity in the waves if we were about to die and lust didn't seem surprising.

* * *

It occurs to me as I wake recently that the one who
was driving too fast must, by now, be dead.
Too late, then, for any exchange with him.
He whose driving allowed such impact from your
stationary start had a record of reckless driving.
So what kind of man would then fight, as if innocent,
for damage to his car and being delayed for a crucial
meeting?
Did he have a wife to lose? And children?
Today I wish I knew.

*

It was beside the sinking boat I witnessed tangles of
guilt and heard why you were driving that car at all, its
gearbox faulty though you didn't know. But stories of
the accident, and last few days, believable as they
might be, were not the act of dying: you had moved
outside tales of living. At last that fact sank in.

iv.

Under a hostel sheet something seemed stark.
At birth I came through you before living within your
orbit, and that was renewed at sea.
But having re-found I was sent back up, leaving you
to the deep. To separate and breathe, to leave you, to
live, was not a choice but the path was set. Whether
to death or life, I could only submit.
Those moments of seeing my life and looking into
light, mocked old notions of knowing.

This awakening had been at sea and I had no wish to lose it, not a second time.

I spread a sheet of sanctuary and crept in, shutting out a threatening chorus of demand: "What is the matter? What happened? What happened?"

While I arrived in search of a sheet, thinking only of the emptiness beneath, they tug, tugged me, shaping me for newsy stories. "Weren't you scared? Were there sharks? How far did you swim?" I had not come where I mattered least for such thrusted questioning.

* *

Waking to the morning, grateful for the clarity of day it is easy to lose the strangeness of night. But in this short interlude there was no wish to scramble back to the familiar. Something had been given and given at sea. If I did run to have a story, any story of it, there would be a loss.

To move from sea to land was the task set before me, but to be land locked too soon seemed to be a threat, not understood by those who believed I required diversion. They offered to help me forget, while I wished to remember. And there was no question of going home to once more horrify father. Besides, my attachment to him kept me from the solitude in which to finally comprehend that you had passed where I could not yet follow.

* *

Words in plenty have since danced round that motionless exhaustion. In later years I was to say "I went to look for her and did find my mother, though not as I expected." The visit in search of a dead mother became a subject for hairdressers, or brought out at a party to someone I didn't know. What had silenced me was later turned to chatter.

"Come for sherry, tell me about it," encouraged the warden at the time.

"It never helps to bottle things up," declared the doctor, coming to treat me for shock.

It never occurred to me either of them might know my way for me. Although dropping to speechlessness, was hardly exercising a choice, there was neither panic nor call for rescue.

It was knowingness which had been shown up, being silent was not the problem. However, once convinced something should be done, others could easily win with a socially acceptable threat and force to follow: a threat finally sufficient to send me leaping back to words.

A defeat to linger – their judgement taken in beneath the skin.

* *

In the first line of medical scrutiny immediately after the incident, doctors were ready to wipe out deep sea treasures with a cheerful "swallow these, you are suffering from exposure and trauma."

"Leave me, please leave it for me."

My protest shouted emphatically was further proof of need.

Back where I had a student room, of course I knew that the boat tipped up in suddenly rough sea, yet I had been with the mother I'd gone to seek and there had been a haunting light where I'd not quite drowned. "Accident" hardly seemed the word to encompass that.

And how was I to speak of what unfurled at sea? How was it to be brought ashore without becoming ridiculous? Not easily and not in the school-clever phrases I'd grown into using.

It made full sense when I had only to go with it, yet nothing carried me now.

I lay in shallows, brought in to the edge and beached - the force that had taken me to shore quite gone, along with that light, exquisite, soft and golden white.

To curl around the absence was to not entirely lose or betray.

The edge of its shadow might be all that remained but it seemed a state of grace to lie in a bath and stay dissolved in its haze.

* *

Was it several weeks later when sun came to the window, not summer's draining heat but a gentle autumnal gift? With the hostel vacant of students for the morning, perhaps it was safe to tiptoe to the warmth. Outside the sky was surprisingly high. On my way to a hillside graveyard, colouring leaves were absorbing. I lay on a stone barely warmed by the crisp, light sun, on top of the grave, not below; it was relief to, at last, feel certain mother was dead and I was alive. And looking up into the vast and opened sky there was room for all I did not yet understand. Out here in the open what I could not comprehend did not close me in. Suspended hours passed. It was chilled early evening before I rose, then paused; it could be birdsong that courting, cooing and a

40

responding, asking nothing but delight. A smile spread for the couple behind a nearby grave whose words were not wood-pecking brittle, but only for sweet exchange. It made a dolphin of me, no longer of the water alone but able to play near land. Old songs surged through me as I ran down the hill and at the hostel door I surprised a student with a hug.

"No one knew you were going out. What have you been up to?"

"Turning dolphin – a dolphin and all will be well."

Soon enough it was obvious that this cheer was far from adequate, but relief and readiness for bed kept me from care.

I had not realised that, in my day of absence, pills under the bed were discovered.

*

I woke to see a net had been prepared. The three walked in and I knew to jump while voices continued, an orchestrated chorus of agreement, "professional help," "looked after" and, of course, "proper rest." Taken away to be at their mercy, but they would take control decently and smiled at the end of my bed. "You can trust us," they said. If I screamed it could only prove them correct. Besides, who would come to protect if mother was dead? These were the powerful and they had had enough. I leapt out, pulling on a jacket, they had come fully dressed, while I faced them alone in flimsy night clothes. "I'm fine and going to classes today," I declared.

Pursued, I left once more the wealth of the seashore.

By attending classes and passing exams I could prove myself, even so it was the territory of judgement, where the judges were never fully revealed. And what if it had been a madness that gripped?

Much vanished from sight. The tide of hope went far out and a fog of doubt closed in.

I could move with surprising assurance along the set paths, "doing very well," so they said. But what was no longer in focus, hovered at the edge of attention, or sat as deep dread in the gut.

v.

I fought once I saw I must and seemed to win, diverting their gaze by doing okay at university.

If I banged my head against a wall occasionally, in frustration at being shut out from myself, this did not let me back in.

I had excuses but knew something precious was gone, the way back to it forgotten.

Something went dormant. It was a period where I barely dreamt.

Finding words springing to life, flaming then dying out, also shut down and I no longer wrote. Of course, I never intended to lose so much. I didn't mean to find myself stuck in lists of things to do, and obligations, cut off from playful writing.

It would be six years before I sought a different kind of sanctuary and began to recall detail.

* * *

We are struggling to keep afloat, caught in inexorable motion, when suddenly we agree my mother is present. Dropping to where she is about me, blood pulsing – sinking deeper, heart and breath seem becalmed to shimmering rainbow – before all colour fuses in that extraordinary light! Where did conviction surge from that I'd ached for this all my life?

Without a separate heartbeat – without the beat of time –I lay within a promise of forever.

A full blooded scroll unrolled – a showing of necessity that I could only be there. Amazed that days on the way had not been as luminous, I stood at the peak of all that had been. But it began to re-roll, squeezing me into certainty: you are to go back down, to go through it again!

Prized light vanished as I shot up again beside the sunken boat. Only the voiceless command remained: Do not look back! Swim for it and do not turn! I did pause to surprise the four. "I will swim," I told them, whereas before I had been adamant I could never make it to that far shore and none of them could swim at all.

*

Once I did look back to see if the others were still afloat; nothing was visible, a rough wave crashed in my face, panic set in - "I can't do this. I can't live if they do not."

"Do not look back," had been the command. Surrendering to movement again, I reached rocks.

And there, hidden sheltering in a bay, was a boat with fishermen, mending nets, waiting for the storm to pass.

It was then I turned, hungering to find the light.

How could I have done it! How could I have left such

peace? Forgetting it had not been a choice; having been taken deep into the sea and brought to shore by a will I could not claim as my own, I was left washed up with flotsam; in the foam and junk at the edge.

*

With binoculars the fishermen saw an orange lifejacket and went to help. When eventually they came near to me again they bellowed out. I couldn't hear but thought they had only two of the four on board.
I could not face it if one of the three men and the little girl were drowned.
From a rock I flung myself.
Perhaps I assumed the body would shatter to bits.
It didn't of course. From such a height I could hardly hope to splatter; there were only cuts and gashes.

*

I was lying where I'd thrown myself when the fishermen came back. They weren't offering rescue, they could not come in on rocks. I had to swim out to them and found the girl vomiting, the man who had been bleeding in the water out cold. Both had been in the boat all along. The fishermen had gone back to mark the sunken wreck with a buoy. They dropped us at a bay, where there were people in the distance, and hurried off again in case the boat might yet be saved. I carried the seven year old down the jetty, two young men carried the injured man. When we could take them no further we laid them on dry sand. No one hurried to help. We were more or less naked, having long before ripped off sodden clothing, but it was the helplessness I was ashamed of, as I went for assistance. "Please, I'm so sorry, but can you help?" I addressed myself to a woman and passed out.

Someone must have carried me as I failed to carry the child.

*

My mother's friend, a woman of fifty, was throwing herself at my feet. I'd never seen an adult prostrate. And if I was shaky myself, how could I possibly help her to stand? She was distraught. Apparently she'd put toll calls through to father several times, then cancelled each. She could not tell him what she adamantly believed that I, too, had died as her guest. When we failed to return she plagued the police with enquiries about crashes, but never thought to say we'd been out in a boat. Mother's friend lay collapsed and reduced on the floor and "it's all right, father need never know," was all I could think to say.

What had I done that this grown woman should be beside herself before me?

*

The three men with whom I'd shared what we took to be the last of life, when we'd said the strangest things at each gasped breath, lingered not wanting separate rooms. We stayed close, perhaps if we parted it might be too much to face each other again.

I overheard the sobbing mother ask, "Did she leave my daughter when she swam? Why didn't she take her?"

The accusation echoed, full volume. I wasn't what she thought, I was not my life-saving sisters, strong swimmers with certificates. Mother, in bragging of badges, medals and considerable prowess in her family, must never have added that one would be of little use in water. Once more I was the one least wanted here.

I had cherished hopes of sacrifice to prove my worth, but my own expectations of rescue had always been on land, perhaps children on the railway I'd run to save. I'd not ever dreamt a rescue at sea. And that drive for survival just came alive. The brothers defended my actions but their mother's cry denounced. True, despite initial terror, I behaved reasonably, if not bravely and hadn't taken the only life jacket off the little girl, when offered it at the start, for a swim to shore. Besides I could not swim what I took to be miles of sea, with a 7 year old on my back. But that was not the point: I was not heroic. I had not set out to save anyone, simply followed a voice that came through. This was a puzzling new face to that serious offence of "selfish" we had been so trained against. I had simply swum, leaving a girl who was ten years younger; I had obeyed a voice and gone alone. Some saw rescue in the episode, but a heroine I knew I was not. And I felt that if any who believed in me really knew how totally incidental any rescuing had been to my swim, they too must be ashamed. A sheet kept out humiliation and the mother's cry, for under it was no judgement of the force which had taken me and seemed not mine to give away, not even in heroics.

*

Old expectations of myself lay shattered.
So perhaps the doctors who called it shock were correct, if I was shocked out of complacency. Perhaps I knew nothing, or had it all wrong? One thing seemed certain – that I had been carried at sea. But was it some current, taking us along the river of our lives, back to oblivion at sea? Was "it" best forgotten? And the light? What was I to make of that?
Nothing yet, not outside of a sheet, for out there old voices waited: "cut the spiritual stuff, who do you think you are?" "Dying mothers are commonplace, just get on with it and make less fuss." Invitations in plenty, everywhere, were to forget and let it sink back to the sea bed leaving little trace.
The gift of life re-given could stay miraculous only beneath a silent sheet.

* * *

Your presence permeated every cell as I sank and felt surrounded.
Our contact then seemed absolute and oceanic.
But then I was nearly drowning.

It turned golden white at the dark tunnel's end,
where you slid into light and I could not follow.
I was stopped and that was final!

vi.

Who can speak that move out of water into air, and shaping up on earth with talk?

What hope of bringing water to shape: surf might rise and fall but keeps no form.

It washes back against the rocks of shore. At sea the sea seems limitless.

And once we move into words the unspeakable is separate, left at the edge, hovering just out of reach and faintly threatening.

Perhaps I wished, a second time, for that slow process in moving into speech, wishing to linger, as after birth, before joining in the talking.

I had no notion I might be at the mercy of psychiatrists, who could insist on drugging or keeping me. Mother would never have tolerated any upstart having the audacity to know better about her daughters.

* * *

Even when you found my ways unfamiliar, you gave full shelter.

No one else should presume the right to find me faulty while you lived.

Those too ready to decide what must be good for me, fine-tuned old resistance - I was not one to hand myself, or my understanding, over for anyone else's management.

vii.

I wished to stay with the sea; it and I had dealings with each other long before.

Wave upon wave of reconnection took me back - being of the ocean as well as the family.

Beyond the small town 1950s colonial life was always the wild surf, which crashed against high cliffs and claimed grown men.

The precarious belonged with the sea.

Even landlocked days kept a watery edge, liquid from which we emerged. It was there in perpetual motion, the power beyond the confines of town.

* * *

A childhood at the sea side - beware of falling rocks - beware of falling. It is not just that the cliffs are high and sheer, they are unreliable. Adults always yell to be careful. Where substantial land is at its end is obvious from the top: yet that is treacherous. Below, full tide pounds against the cliff and when waves recede, the curve of erosion can be seen. Beneath that solid edge is emptiness waiting to break.

When the sea lies far out it leaves sun-warmed pools, where crabs appear and children grab them, the long vast stretch of grey to black sand shows itself and massive rocks are beached. Great fallen trunks bleached bright and skeletal lie at unlikely angles.

Broken rocks, crabs and bits of shell are sharp on feet but the pools are ours. The biggest, farthest pool, left between rocks black with mussel, is ideal for swimming. That is agreed, yet there is still the threatening, "Don't ever go in without us!"

Later in the day when the sea is back in and hard rocks hidden again, it's better to swim further down, at Snapper Bay, a perfect place for body surfing. It is time to move, the rules are given and no one need mention that if you stayed here to swim, the full force

49

of incoming tide might smash your brains open on a stone.

"How lucky the children are to play all summer on the beach" – sand castles – bare feet running free and healthy sea air – a river that widens out below good diving cliffs to a suitable swimming hole just the right width. A constant basin, yet the river is always moving, as you can see at its rocky, narrowed, ocean-going exit.

"Once it gets to the sea can it ever be a river again?"

"Do get undressed!"

There is the tug of the sea – a pull to merge with ocean. The sea need only wait to take a river to oblivion but some days it is less patient and comes up the river bed, "might it also come too soon for us?" Sometimes it came for fishermen and took them.

When I could only say "I don't want the sea to take me yet" there was general laughter.

*

A blazing fire of driftwood gathers us - faces nearly scorched. We huddle and sing but first the sea's spoils: fishermen might bring a snapper or kahawai but even we collect mussels to be laid on a spare sheet of roofing iron. Local Maoris have shown where paua is best found, those black slugs whose shimmer of blue-green shell is hidden behind them, but they lie too deep for us; only the determined go out waist deep at special tides. You need a strong knife to prise them from their tough, substantial grasp and more effort is required to get the shell off, exposing their pale underside. When the remains are scrubbed away there is the splendour of a shining shell.

* * *

Inexorable movement is the backdrop. We were born into lives in progress, brothers, sisters, aunts, mothers, fathers and the cousins, lives which didn't stop despite the shock of our beginning. We drop to sleep to the moving sea and wake to its motion. It lay about the bach[1], audible and never absent, if forgotten.

*

Each night as we gave up our daily upright stand, we sank where sea rolled through our sleep; it was in us and we were at sea. When wave upon wave streamed through it was easy to flow with them.

By day father and mother might be the inevitable and protective top and bottom of a huge clam shell. Yet there was always an open sea.

From our shell you could see out to vast expanse, but there remained some threat that if the shell closed too tight to seal us in, it would shut out our ocean.

*

We moved into a surprisingly solid place on earth with sturdy limbs but close behind and shadowing lay the water's edge. Each knew it differently and mostly it went unspoken, though one important cousin told

---

[1] Our bach was six miles from home, which seemed a considerable distance. We went regularly at weekends and stayed through the long summer. It was basic with its long drop toilet, way at the bottom of a big garden, past rustling bamboo.

me his certainty that all his life's dreams were in that light at birth. "They aren't lost. One by one those dreams come and I know it's important if it has golden light," he said. For him there was confidence that pieces of light ahead would be found. I knew with less certainty light which had been complete was now in fragments, for my tale of arrival was of lightning bringing power lines down; a story of scattered light.

*

The game of siblings may be tough but being born into a game in play there is no stopping, despite sometimes longing to let go, relieved of jostling – "whose team?" – "whose turn?" – to be swaddled and sealed in again. The youngest sister, swimming before she could walk, was a fish, and highly praised for it, while I, as a changeling thing, had to scramble from sea back to land. I tried to warn her but she still went right across the river on a dribbling, mournful St Bernard. In my attempts to scare her I frightened only myself. It seemed the adults left me to the ocean. Its meaning, coming to visibility like seaweed at low tide, became tangled into me.

One black wave stayed and was a comfort. It might be dark yet came as a gift of light. "Ride" was its warning, "ride it with open arms, since if you resist there is only pounding, breaking surf." It was difficult to ride out wanting a mother who was so busy.

She was the water from which I emerged yet I could get stuck, post birth, under waves crashing over.

Parents left for a funeral one wet morning and didn't forbid the sea. They incanted the rules of the beach year in year out but probably it didn't occur to them their teenage daughters could consider swimming this dismal day. It wasn't just a swim that was proposed. To go in without an adult was to diminish parental authority but it was the sea itself we'd pit ourselves against in diving for mussels at high tide.

As we ran to the edge, throwing jerseys on a log, I knew this challenge was not for me; it was not for me to follow a sister and yet I could not stop. A powerful swimmer, confident in water and already outrageous as she tested good looks and new powers, this sister was out in front, had been in front all my life and would be followed as always. She had moved into adolescence while I was at its edge. Simply to go after her was foolish I knew, even as I dived, but to pull back seemed not possible.

For me the sea should never be defied, it was greater, even if for my sister it was a power against which to test increasing strength.

What happened in the water is unsure. The river, now a ripping current beneath surf at high tide, caught me. I told them afterwards, perhaps correctly, though probably out of pride, that I had been stunned swimming through a breaker straight into a black rock. Then the pull caught me. But I wasn't clear what was really true except my failure: I had been unable to get myself out.

I don't remember her arms reaching me, though recall a sharp threat for when the sister I had too easily imagined boundless was at the limit of her strength, she turned fierce. Once safely in and put to bed, I came to with brandy down the throat and another threat, "don't you dare tell!" Of course not! I'd had a lifetime surviving as a sibling, besides, what was there to tell?

If I were to say "I owe my life to my sister" she would only tease, "she's at her exaggerations again."

We'd had a fright but no one was dead, and the daily news was full of more important rescuing. Yet having been life-saved I felt out of my depth. Long after being brought to shore I floundered.

If each night in sleep I went back again and again to the water, might I get out on my own? My dreaming held the promise of it, as creatures came enticing me back to sea and soon there were also absorbing patterns with numbers.

Meanwhile, recurring temperatures and blocked nasal passages were to be tackled. I was unconcerned with the doctor's opinion until I realised I was to be handed over to him. "With these tonsils out of the way, my girl, we'll build you up again."

I felt awash and waterlogged, but did they intend to cut me out because I had failed to get myself from the ocean and was now taking too long to find the way to extricate myself?

Clarity came late and what a laugh it gave them: I was sinking when panic rose, "stop holding me under!" Ducking had always been forbidden, my shouted outrage entirely justified. A nurse, turning to the noise, saw me, already drugged for the surgeon's cut, start up and bolt.

"Never had I chased a patient before though my father did in days when tonsils came out on the kitchen table," the doctor told me afterwards, repeating it over the years, it was always a good joke.

I came round, after the operation, to haemorrhage and deteriorating health, not the promised improvement.

"You've come too late," I said into the wall, my back turned on both parents, those first visitors.

I knew now the power of brute force. I had not kept well but had kept belief that there was a route out. Having been held under, hope drowned. And the dreams stopped; my soul had always given mother trouble, had they now cut it away?

* * *

It was you I woke that night at Urenui Beach. It was inconceivable to disturb and worry him but you liked adventures.

Having been unable to put my head under, the rest of that holiday following my fright, I was suddenly awake in the tent, certain I should not leave next day still unable to do it.

You didn't question my request but gathered a towel and we walked companionably in silence.

Finally I went beneath a salty river, not the surf, and came up gasping.

One memory has you walking in to me.

But did I ever see you enter water forwards?

Certainly there were other late night naked swims.

The other memory has you sitting on the sand holding a towel for me.

What is sure is that you didn't ask anything and I assumed you knew nothing of what had occurred in your absence.

It would be several years after your death before I talked to him and he was amazed, "Of course we knew! How could you imagine you kept it hidden? People saw you being dragged back to the bach but since, by the time of our return, you were all subdued there seemed no need to reprimand."

That was also the time he told of his nightmares after I turned my back with, "You've come too late!"

The tone of my voice, then, still gave him a chill. He could not forget the despairing 13 year old me I barely recalled.

Perhaps it wasn't surprising that, after the tonsil and haemorrhage episode, he finally took over and said, "No more doctors and no more school until she is ready." I took this protection from further surgery, for sinus polyps this time, which doctors at a city hospital recommended, as one of his most loving gestures.

You stopped taking me to medical appointments and I stayed at home a while, teaching myself algebra from books.

The precious number dreams might have stopped with the anaesthetic, but numbers as symbols were still absorbing.

That was until the mathematics teacher, a recent arrival from Ireland with a beautiful wife, bewildered by our town, arrived at the house telling you and me that the algebra must stop. I'd gone too far with it, he said, and was overheating my brain. Perhaps my dreams in the margin alarmed him. He didn't say, for somehow we all accepted with no further comment, that he could take away all the books.

That next time I was in trouble at sea, visiting the South Island, five of us had simply been sitting talking on a large boat. It was new to them and tipped over completely. When the mother I'd gone to seek seemed unmistakeably present, I wasn't the one to cry out this conviction, though I alone sank with relief.
Odd how I spent so long straining against enclosure while she lived, yet surrendered utterly.
I can claim to have found her, but that is only a statement of belief in what then seemed certainty; to describe may be only parading faith, except that surfacing from the deep I swam. When fresh and not exhausted, I was sure I couldn't make it. After nearly drowning, with no will I recognised as mine, my swim, to the nearest shoreline I couldn't even see, was unnervingly direct.

* * *

I can't say it was "my will" to live – it simply came and took me.

You were the one with Christian faith yet in my teenage years there was soul wondering.
Though it took your dying to bring home how far I failed to accept non-existence.
That remained beyond my living comprehension.

The demand was decisive: "You are to go through it again!" It didn't add "and this time do not forget" but I was in no doubt this was the implication.

Clarity cut through straight and clear. Later, those others who didn't share the call felt able to assert what was good for me, felt entitled to override those most precious moments when thought came with a leap and was fully connected to me.

*

"You were impossible, I came back and you barely spoke until you declared yourself a dolphin. How could we know you weren't about to drown yourself?"

But my roommate was a "we" in that anxiety, standing firmly with the warden and making no move to comprehend if water and silence made sense. "I was your friend and you did not trust me," was all I could say.

"You should have explained."

"There was no vantage point from which to view and toss you an account of myself!"

We were friends yet it took years of absence before we spoke. I was still in a fight for vindication. It was not just the silent figure on the bed I would gather to cohesion; in arguing my case I inclined to imposing purity of purpose on my path and reduced to paper-thin those who wanted me back in usual clothes and back in a familiar state of mind. Turmoil had dogged my previous year and no doubt friends were fed up. After all there had been that earlier return to the docks, where we had waved off my mother on the ferry. Locked memory got on the move when I went back there, bringing me more alive to myself than had seemed possible since her death. It felt a relief but those around were perturbed.

I simply thought - "They think I haven't the courage for what has happened," whereas I had not, then, lost my nerve.

*

Perhaps it was unexpected when I baulked at stepping from the sheet and getting up to words. I'd been articulate and usually left a trail of talk.

But whatever happened in Christchurch was not an everyday event for which there was vocabulary at the ready. It seemed obvious I needed to wait for sentences to shape. Curled out of the world but not against myself, I lay in what might unfold.

As for that lost expectation of proving myself with bravery, nursed through adolescence - it would take years before there would be comfort in other myths, of Orpheus also told not to look back.

ix.

While there was visceral conviction that you were gone from me,
gone from my touch and smell,
your vivid presence gone where I could not go,
there was no word to say.

Later on I would know that, though sadness can get its grip on every cell, the relentless does not continue. You slip back in to using words.

*

My sense of reunion with you was ended. I was washed up with only bits, after what had seemed a complete, drowning into light.
Why had I swum for life to be a body which looked whole, if understanding stayed so fragmented?
And trying to assert just another near death experience proved what can't be shared.

*

No-one else stopped in amazement. They had "luck" and "chance" or at best "uncanny" to account for it.
But for me it was definite: no "I" was in place to make that swim when already exhausted and with no notion of which way to go since shore remained invisible.
I found myself on a rocky promontory with dread of losing that force which had taken me.

* * *

The pulse of the sea, which was always there at the heart of things, though at the periphery of town, now fades into tales of its existence, its elusiveness no longer lived.
When the sea has no force except in the pitfalls of the human mind, then we are stranded, high and dry.

C

"Stupidity consists in wanting to reach conclusions.
We are a thread and expect to know the whole cloth."
Flaubert

i.

I sought something of you.
When I headed south, above all I wanted your death
to seem real.
And real is what I got.
But I also went to the city you came from, a place I
didn't know, since you had friends there and I wished
to hear what they had to say.

* * *

I went to look for you in Christchurch and, across the
world, kept seeking; enclosed in London far from
ocean, I sought what once connected me to you. And
do see you, sometimes, standing in that black evening

dress, the one shot with gold and silver thread glistening as if sequinned, low at the neck, full from the waist. I was enchanted then but some magic passes. Year after year there was the tree decked in glory surrounded by parcels on Christmas morning– its unreal sheen – the unaccountable plenty – until having seen suddenly that presents must have been stacked elsewhere and added in the night, that year wanted none of it, not one single gift. Your radiance was less abruptly shed, perhaps it simply faded, but loss from withering is no easier to forgive.

As you left on the ferry you waved and called but when you went finally there was no farewell, an unlikely departure from you who liked a grand occasion and stood your ground in a scene. I stare at your photo on the wall, at your straight black hair before it was permed; once I simply ran towards you.

You, who had been woven into me, I began to seek in information, though collected facts did not bring back the power of smell, or that lost feel of flesh. Still there were questions to ask your friends and sisters, so I heard how ready you were to flirt and of the engagement you announced on your sister's wedding day, when you had already made eyes for a time at her groom. I pull fragments into view and puzzle how and when I mislaid so much of you.

ii.

You became an object to catch, subject to untrustworthy description.
While living you had not been reducible to my shifting gaze, from admiring to flashing fury.

Your life you knew as I did not, but you left us to it, to take hold of your image as we chose.

Ours was not a culture with a rich mourning tradition. We "got on", difficulties were overcome, with cemeteries kept to the margins, out of town.

When a cousin's Maori husband was killed, seven months after you, there was a spurt of outrage - that the Maori had far better rituals and we didn't have them.

But my complaint was also personal, that you bequeathed a sorrow I didn't want, when navigating sadness was not where you'd been any help.

You preferred your children in sunshine with smiles.

Yet you, too, must have known the inevitability of human grief.

*

The brass on our front door and step were kept at a high shine.

Though night must follow day, bright light was kept on in front of us (and dark shadows stayed across the road with a suffering neighbour).

You danced your '50s cheer, convinced the grim need not appear before children.

Then it did.

It wasn't easy to accommodate that even the sun can be eclipsed.

*

How far was it a matter of temperament, yours different from my own?

And through my teens was still caught in taste for melodrama, even if not entirely believing in whatever stirred great sighs.

Then undoubtedly sadness sunk its teeth into me, it had bite, though, above all, your death confounded.

iii.

While you lived, you were simply central and standing firm. You were to grow within and live beside, not one to discuss.

Once our being together finished, perhaps I thought it possible words might catch all that was missing.

Was it your crash which broke apparent cohesion into pieces?

*

Your friends resorted to hyperbole.

Idealised virtues baffled but since no one spoke like that of the living, you must be dead, I supposed.

* * *

There were a few accounts while she was alive.

"Not one of you girls are a patch on your mother," a chemistry teacher declared.

Others also spoke of parties when she arrived in town. "Boy, did she know how to let her hair down!"

I knew the can-can and pot lid dancing, from creeping to watch, and had seen her lack of sympathy for the restraint in some "gentility."

I sought who she had been from selective memories: from the day she adamantly wouldn't miss the church sale of second hand clothes, despite my lingering illness spots. So I was to stay out of sight under a trestle table.

She flung open the doors to loud embraces, as Maori women from surrounding Pas[2] arrived in busloads.

She paraded in the no longer wanted hats of goodly ladies and laughed loudest as Maori women made a carnival, trying on several dresses at once.

Father, who could do a terrifying Maori haka, helped them apply for benefits and knew about the Maori land trust.

None of this matched what we heard at school.

The mother of a girl I was sent to play with down the road was angry we played with S and had been to her house. "If you go there again I'll have to smack you. It's not a clean place."

At seven I didn't argue but knew it a better scrubbed home than my own. Mother said of S's Maori mother, "That poor woman tries harder than anyone," and she did, S always wore impeccably pressed, starched dresses.

At the beach local Maoris came to collect Mother for a feast. Unlike Father she loved a greasy hangi or the freshest seafood.

---

[2] Maori Pa was where a Maori community continued to live communally.

*

But to us the Maori could also seem unnervingly different, as they sat in tatty jackets, worn faces and quiet dignity, simply waiting out long hours for a bus to return them to the Pa.

Our parents did not rest till work was done and "doing" was definitely the virtue.

*

She got out of town by driving an ambulance or a bus. When driving one team to a city tournament, she stopped at a water melon stall and lined them all for a pip spitting contest. We knew her prowess but after she won so did an admiring Maori girl at school.

*

Any foreign hitch-hikers were brought home. As were the first wave of Japanese tourists, met on our mountain, which rose like Mount Fuji, a cone out of a coastal plane.

She, then, agreed to a Japanese student coming to us, despite the Mayor pointing out there had been lingering war anger over the party she gave the mountaineers. At the time there was pride in her, "It's time we got to know them." Only later I noted she didn't ask if it was those damaged in Japanese prison camps who had objected.

*

Curried fish also came home. She got spices from the Indian greengrocers, then took plenty of fish to exchange for their cooking one for us.
My sense of then is days filled with the flavour of good food.

*

Like most she fitted in and didn't. To me she was the contrast to mothers with a different smell. Strangeness was in other houses.
I was sent to play in one where the mother lay on her sofa, with an over-robust husband at a loss how to cheer her. I took him our artichoke soup, and an occasional strong dish with chilli and garlic.

*

With friends and at other peoples' houses I'd always gone more by my nose, not putting into words how smells and presentation mattered, yet they are readily recalled. One great comfort was that hint of old clothes and coconut oil too long in the cupboard after each deep sniff of father's head.

*

From 10 till she went away at 13, I regularly biked with my special friend through a long summer, to swim in their pool each school lunch time, putting biscuits on the account because her mother wouldn't notice, while mine would be a vigilant hawk.

However, after staying with us this friend told at school how we'd all swum with no clothes. When the teacher made a joking reminder, that even I must bring togs to school, embarrassment was tinged with pride.

*

A family across the road lived by different standards. A new architect designed house of glass and a garden with unexpected tall globe artichokes and aubergine. A style I admired.
The young mother showed me unknown imported coffee beans, their modern New Zealand paintings, and without meaning to showed heavy guilt, a thickening gloom taking hold.
She was no social stalwart but a gentle soul of sorrows, this mother of my sister's friend. She sometimes reached out to me and was surprising. In my teens I was invited to the "film club" meeting in a dark room to see foreign films. As a child I looked, as I left our house, at their two flattened, bulbous jaguars, admiring their distinction.
(It took decades for me to realise the other car in that fatal accident was also a jaguar, yet I had it firmly pictured sleek, long and shark pointed at its front.)

*

In the house of a high school friend the atmosphere felt tight with approvals and disapprovals as ours was not.
The parents were quick to be sharp with each other. But after both praised my having done better than

their daughter, I would not go back! This was dangerous ground we kept away from at home. Competitiveness was played down, never made explicit.

*

Few women worked outside the home and none inspired. They weren't Grace Darling heroic, or as misunderstood as Maggie Tulliver, but a few mothers also taught. It seemed uncomfortable for their children, so it was a relief mine only appeared for sports and plays and parent committees.
Though, once we began our leaving, her not having interesting work loomed as grim.

*

It was a place and time of family life and we regularly included some who weren't in one. Single women maybe, but not the female divorced.
The few whose husbands behaved badly and were humbled won some sympathy but to brazen it out was another matter! What comment when one of those went up to Holy Communion in clacking heels higher than anyone else.

*

I would have to move across the world before hearing anyone call their mother "a good friend," but at University the mother of a student, expected to "talk as an equal" before I was equal to it.

At home I'd shared confidences with two in the year below, at one remove from my orbit. Teenage poetry, usually well hidden beneath the mattress, was shown only to a girl who wanted the boy I fancied.

And after being rescued by my sister, I spoke freely to one other, who also acted, but she told her older sister, who told mine, proving why you were friendly but "kept your counsel" in an enclosed town.

iv.

You might have fed us more imaginatively than most, as we moved to sukiyaki way ahead, and then there was the excitement of getting a freezer to make ice cream, yet to slip out unfed, still light and eager, increasingly appealed before you died.

Afterwards there was inescapable weight.

When your beloved Daddy got sick you learnt to cook to tempt him (this came from your sister; you didn't mention his death, only that he liked to party as you did.)

You continued to cook well for us, for the sick and guests.

You'd have been intrigued by all the ingredients I can get in London.

*

You sent off letters regularly, filling in his family and your own with the wonders of offspring. Though we didn't hear such praise.

Bulletins were posted to Fiji, Hawaii and the US, as well as across New Zealand.

Corals came back, handbags and dolls; new net petticoats and used clothes.

As distant relations they seemed more giving than when they turned up in person, except for his storytelling now-American sister, who made exciting returns to show there wasn't only one way of doing. That she came with scarlet nails yet was clearly "a lady" put your mantra in doubt – at six this was just one further unanswered question.

*

It was a different era and not one of praising children, though there was ready affirmation for "being helpful".

School was for correcting faults – spelling and punctuation. Mistakes were their only interest in composition and mine went on too long.

So perhaps it's not surprising a gem from childhood shone out, has been returned to and kept its gleam.

The headmaster's wife only taught if usual staff were sick. This day, as she came in, she said, "Oh, it's this class! Good, I'll get another of your long stories, Barbara."

*

I have no memory of taking writing to you yet, for a while, left any we could take home in the letterbox of an old woman I didn't know.

I'd put my shoes in her unused milk box so I, too, could arrive at school barefoot and she didn't give me away.

She seemed to have no existence in your network until that day she met me crying and I said you were making me go to school though I had the measles.

In fact the school pet mice were dead in our shed because you wouldn't have them in the house. You didn't like mice. The cat did and knocked the cage to the ground.

After I got home to your outrage over the measles story, my old woman "friend," having lost her potency, got no further poetry from me.

*

I had not realised what you spread by letter – you played down praise and agreed with father that we must all be treated the same. No fuss made of one for anything.

So I was unaware my acting success gave pleasure. I'd had to fight to begin, wearing down your insistence on piano lessons, not the stage, for decent girls, then took for granted my ability was not personal, it simply came down from his acting family.

Given how it satisfied, it is marked that, after your death, I did not act again. Not once.

Was it that with trust shaved off our lives, I could not quite trust myself? Or had I put myself on display in any part until it felt as if our family was too visible and I didn't like it?

Though I also moved away to where there were professional theatres.

Besides, by then, I wanted to write the script, not just be in those already written.

* * *

The problem of being "known about" pervades a small community and we became the subject.

He did not like gossip and you, apparently, concurred. Most scandal was unpleasant and best left unsaid, it gave an illusion of knowing more than you really did, he said.

Yet your mother, who grew brittle with age and widowhood, rigid in her entitlements, became a carping prattle and cross you didn't dish any dirt on your husband.

*

Years later your eldest sister became outspoken, though her slip into senility was blamed.

"Who was he?" That one to pluck the flower of the family then bury her in the country? A small man to take on a strapping girl, "He made fuss as if she was some princess. Tea in bed for a strong lass, how absurd is that?"

"You know the one, who whisked her off and fathered too many children, leaving her insufficient time for sisters."

While you were alive, loyalty to him disappointed them, but your dying left more space for their criticism.

*

One major complaint was his coming home for a simple lunch he was happy to make himself.

A proper man, like your father, was away from home long days and many nights.
Ours liked being home and being able to help, boiling up nappies before work in days before a clunking washing machine with its hand wringer.
He didn't hang them up, however, as the neighbours might see.

*

Though family-minded, its history was not what you shared, except one tale of father pictured as the best, self-sacrificing to educate two younger brothers and to help his mother.
You never gave the context – his dubious, gambling actor father – just as you failed to mention your own feuding sister, or your mother's extreme behaviour towards her firstborn.
Offered only noble images of family life, I had to wait for the distant aunt to glean gritty detail to make sense of absorbed tensions.

*

And in houses with photographs of young men killed in war before producing children, we partially filled a vacancy with fake grandparents; your warm father being dead and your cold mother fortunately far away, you sought substitutes, and so we went to tea.
The one with lace as well as loss, who had the delicacy of her finest china and a treasure trunk, appears in dreams. The other didn't appeal.
We called them Granny and I knew we were only there because the young men in uniform, who sat on

a piano and hung in the hall, were not, though no one ever said so.

v.

Any sense of who you were and how we lived together became inextricably mixed with your exit.
My flesh began as part of you, though I no longer liked to think of that, having grown squeamish.
I could not go where you had gone, unless by wilful destruction.
Your crash bred muddle over what was you and what must just be me.
But I took up something of your place with father, talking over family concerns.

*

You structured days, you were through my way of being and not entirely a separate presence.
I had not yet begun to come and go with ease. Your taking care had seemed solidly there for me, yet dead you grew elusive.
Whether I even liked you, whether I was determined to be a different kind of woman, you and I were tied far more than I recognised.
By mid-teens your dimpled and ample thighs had me pulling faces.
I wouldn't be like that!
Yet this firm stand turned wobbly. Whatever I took myself to be, I was also and definitely one of your daughters.

You, who kept red polish from my nails, left me to choose scarlet, green or purple.

You, who made sure there were three vegetables and protein, set me to deny the flesh if years of good care were put in question. Protection lay exposed as phony – how could we be kept safe if you could be so broken?

You also cut me loose to buy my first shop-made dress. I chose ugly pastel crimplene.

And it proved only an illusion of new freedoms if your death also kept some grip far stronger than your claiming embrace.

* * *

When she came in a glittering splendour of sequins, promising to bring home a treat from the ball, or to leave magical raisins beside my pillow, I'd have sworn permanent allegiance to her court and there was no doubt she was a fitting Queen; on more motley days I was less sure. If father watched us with tenderness there was fierceness in her. She would fight for us but also fight us.

Without TV and mostly local news, a small town was all I could see, until a school trip at seventeen. After it I marked off the weeks before I could return to films, theatre, music and a city. How could father, having known all that, have deprived me of it? It had been his world, his parents both artists, yet he had moved to a small town, as he turned his heart from his selfish, theatrical father. He opted out of the cruel city of the depression, for a simpler, near self-sufficient life where he would feed his family. We could make our own entertainments in a small community and take responsibility for one another in hard times. Besides, behaviour was visible to all, unlike in the city where greed or self-interest could be better hidden, with professionals doing the dirty work. Father would never have kept me in the life he'd chosen, he expected independence and spirited daughters. The tie to and from mother was less clear.

*

She liked a tight team and took us with her zest for being in the midst of whatever she joined. This included the church, though father was agnostic, and so we were confirmed.

Some months after my confirmation I decided to write to the Bishop requesting he un-confirm me.

It occurs to me, years later, that she helped get the address but asked only one question – whether I was about to refuse my team role of attending church with the family, even at Easter and Christmas? Would I make a scene?

When I baulked at her suggestions for my future, wishing to go far from home to university, her condition was my getting a place in the Christian hostel. References were sent from our vicar and church warden but when I arrived at the interview there was the aged Bishop.

Surely he got hundreds of similar letters, he'd never remember mine?

Even so, when he said my character was highly praised but only my family's involvement in the Church was mentioned, I gulped and repeated what

I'd written to him, that I only had any sense of what God might mean from the sea.

"I thought so," he smiled. "I seem to remember a letter. Never had another like it!"

* *

If you'd stayed present to the power shift which had begun, how might that have been?

But I was left apparently free of you while at the mercy of abrupt absence.

Words my only a weapon against feeling too reduced and ineffective. Words had been initiating challenge while you lived, despite a sister's advice not to argue, when climbing out the bedroom window was simpler.

* *

Quite what I was doing in writing of you, I often asked, and assumed, once I knew that answer, I might stop.

I took for granted I'd never write of father. He was there to enjoy, so there was no need. Besides, the ease of love for him was too rich to try and pin.

Taking hold of a moving life and pulling it from complexity might be a harsh act.

But yours was ended and if my words take you by the throat, is it getting my own back for having been a child you could grab and shake?

*

Sometimes cascading hurt words poured out as if some bottle was tipped over.

Similar phrases dropped onto paper repeatedly, yet each occasion felt like the first formulation of a wounding.

Other days I wake and there is a bubbling up to send your way.
Your dream presence may vanish into day, leaving language briefly on automatic, words as free flowing as desire. Perhaps I might catch sufficient to simply whisper and hear you repeat back, "I love you."
Yet could not quite get there.
Only as this writing comes to an end is it clear that to claim "I love you," as I began to do with him and as is fashionable, would be strange. That was not what was spoken back when we lived side by side.

* *

Hopes of healing, and my belief in woven meaning, took decades to lay extinguished.
Now that capturing your life, or death, in my word net is no longer an option, it's obvious how much must stay unsaid between us[3].
Though I still wonder if, like others, I too will cry for "mother" in my own death throes?

---

[3]Since you kept your age even from best friends and father's courtesy kept it off your stone, when I turned to astrology's patterns I had the wrong chart, making you a double Leo.

When a recent family tree revealed your birth year, giving you an Aries moon, it was startling to see your Neptune on my Cancerian sun, for Neptune is in these notes, from early idealisation, to lack of clarity between us, except in near drowning, and in that theme of escape. It suggests that maybe I am seeing the limited amount there is for me to know.

Meanwhile there is talking of you between being born and dying.

vi.

There was pale plastic primrose on your feet for hot sand and rocks.

Those thickened thighs seemed powerful as we flew as butterflies about your flowering. As caterpillars we spun onto your stem and hung, but were we the same species beating heart near heart?

We lived together, you cooked, I ate and sometimes admired.

There were moments of closeness, over paper dolls from your childhood and old photograph albums, where you were with various men triumphing at golf – treasures brought down from high in the linen cupboard one illness.

And though I disliked advice, when you showed me how to cleanse and tone, I listened carefully. "Take good care of your skin," you said, "you won't get another, so look after this one."

When I began to do so, heading for 40, I often thought of you.

*

You would accuse when I pulled out of your soft embrace.

At what age did I cease to burrow in your flesh?

Who noted when I stopped joining you in a bath, bony legs alongside soft thighs, or as I backed off from the smell and touch of you, ceasing to curl into your bed, except for birthday rituals? You said I'd always been a wriggler.

But around eleven there was also revelation in a poem.

A call to come away, to leave where I only half belonged, seemed to be an old, old song, whose words I'd finally heard.

There was magic in finding a name. At last I "knew" what had always been, that I was also your "changeling".

*

With him there were quite different lines. I never doubted I was his daughter. I clearly came from his side. Not understanding genes I thought you could choose a single allegiance.

Once, by the front hedge he had just cut, I waited, aged seven, for the water tower to relight. With him that night time did a slow motion trick, a stillness to show what "forever and ever" might mean: it held complete certainty of wanting to be with him.

*

You might have been about me before birth but he became the one I reached towards, first with arms, then words.

He gathered me to rest, flat against his firm, haired chest. There was no sinking in to be absorbed by fleshy breasts.

He had no claim to swallow me back. He was for me, yet distinct.

Even when he was at work, or later when I was absent, he fused with the imaginary, the being I longed to touch, the one it was easiest to love.

With you things could get messy.

Even when I believed myself no longer in your circuit, just waiting to move away, fury could still erupt between us – think of the night I biked off for poison. "I'll show her, I'll show her" my only thought, not that it was life I might forfeit to make my point! That did not occur to me as I pedalled hell bent on destruction. I'd make you sorry that I knew. How the passion flared I no longer recall, only that at sixteen I was equipped with keys to the chemistry lab and knew how to make poisonous gas.

Did I provoke clashes to come up against you, fight being our intimacy? Afterwards we never discussed it.

Yet here I am, still interrogating past moments.

Neither of you were as taken by talking as I seem to have been back then.

Perhaps you'd outgrown it and found my being a "chatterbox" exhausting. You said I asked too many questions, yet it's amazing what I couldn't ask.

He never had a lot to say but on the phone, or when friends came round, you could talk and talk.

I learnt to value eavesdropping, except when I overheard unnerving comments about myself.

You didn't often speak to me.

In a life with little singular care, I jumped at each chance to say my piece, my turn at the table at last.

Not a dialogue with you, just a spot to perform.

Watch me! Listen to me! Words tossed like pebbles into the sea.

vii.

Like most I hatched to a cocoon – added in and
sharing residence, a bedroom, meal routines and
words – ways of doing, ways of saying to grow in us
like structuring bones.

Distant aunts helped define the unit – their letters
marked out an extended belonging.

Born to it, I joined and joined – a fellowship of those
who cheered a school, my siblings and several teams.

*

After a sister spent her savings on songs, we danced
together to Elvis, Hank or Dusty Springfield.

We went from home on separate paths but were
recognised by "family" all over town. And you were
our cheerleader.

Fiercely loyal yourself, you effortlessly rallied us for
the family group, though I never much liked team
sports.

*

We gave him peace at home if work days were
difficult.

Your girls were to put clutter from sight and show
neater faces for ease over sherry.

"This is the life," he'd say on holiday, satisfied with
his choices.

It was the only life we knew but you, who'd been a
flirt, a party, city girl, beating men at golf, were now in
rural retreat.

He showed no urge to slip away except to the red red roof, painted for our protection. There he could get long hours alone.

*

He wanted to stay where he had settled, rooted in his big garden and routines, busy with satisfying work.
Were you reluctantly confined?
Children had been your labour and were beginning to leave.
Was loyalty coming to an end if you wanted something new and even small excursions out provided jubilation?
Your friend in Christchurch and your sister were adamant you were determined to travel. Though how much of your vision did I see through my teenage eyes which were seeking more than the town could provide?

*

Did you want something else?
Some years later I visited where you dreamt of going, and didn't have to die to escape.
Had you gone back to Christchurch wanting a way out?
Perhaps you realised you just might be nailed into your old life, by an unmoving husband and all taking for granted you'd be there, holding up the emptying nest for our departure, cooking again should we choose to return.

We lived in a house I'd always known as "home".
As I grew, I only saw small bits to question, not
seeing clearly what was me; not you, not family.
Fighting off enclosure was as far as I could go.
My craving for open windows didn't suit.
The nearly stultifying sense of being submerged,
hemmed into the full family car, made me desperate
for a window open in the back, though this
apparently stiffened your neck.
You said I "never took the easy route" but it seemed
your death gave me a straight path to freedom, before
I recognised how far from finished it was between us.

* *

Where is the lilt to those early days? Or those songs
you sang which still come flooding in?
I expected to slip past your ways, in those glib hopes
of the '60s, yet heard myself pass on the same songs,
mine out of tune because I'd tried to sing deep with
him, not accepting my voice, like yours, was soprano.
And in giving my children celebrations found the
surge required coming direct from yours.
But by my teens was definitely ambivalent, and
refused to be drawn to your circuit, that last year, to
criticise a challenging sister. I'd not join your sphere
of disapproval as you played out the worst of your
own mother after all.

*

From ten, thanks to a hand-me-down bike, I'd learnt
to circumvent, glad the way out of your reach
expanded.

Puberty brought me back with a jolt. Being a girl was
perfectly factual, yet less acceptable if it meant
growing up to follow you.

"I won't," I said. I will not learn to cook or sew and
never type or be a nurse. I wouldn't even consider the
bolder option of being a teacher.

Resistance rolled out in declaration but what else
might there be? I had no idea.

Though the GP left lingering confusion, when I was
13.

"Not everywhere is the same as here." he said. "In
Russia most doctors are women."

Medicine and Russia seemed to be my daunting
prospect, until a dissection.

On slitting open a foetus filled rabbit, it became an
absolute that slicing life would not be my way to
understand it. That much was seen in a flash.

*

Yet up till seven it seems to have been you I might
become – the family queen, the one our father
adored.

As I chose a costume from a friend's big box I didn't,
then, put on trousers of unfettered pirates from wild
seas but wore grandeur, a startling gown for
Cinderella's Ball, with tacky plastic jewels.

Was it also your attention I sought back then?
Recurring dreams revive the glamorous you, dressed to party, or ready for a ball, his buying an orchid for your shoulder and I identifying with his delight in taking out the regal.
Did his sense of your enchantment fade half as much as mine did?
Did I hanker back to the time when your allure beguiled me, that I often dreamt my place alongside the pair of you at that peak?

ix.

I hoped for simplification once you were dead, expected to know what I thought of you.
Acts of generosity remained – those raisins under the pillow – all those clothes you made with dedication.
But drawing others in around us kept you busy with practicalities – sensitivity to emotional subtleties, or suffering, hardly your element.
It was soup you'd send to the troubled, patience was not offered to them or us. Though you did send daughters running out to protect your winter irises, water-wash thin and delicate. After frost we must bring opening ones in, before bright sun destroyed them.

*

I re-cut flowers as they need it, pleased at how much longer they survive.
You took care of flowers but, along with much else, their share of attention was allotted by routine; each week large vases were filled.

Washing, with someone coming in to iron, had its slot, as did childcare by Plunket rules. How far were those, placed in between us at the start, still blocking a connection?

*

Your impatience cut across my nature and my hair. Long ringlet curls were too much effort, as perhaps was tuning into me.

One sister takes me back to the best of being beside you. She, too, luxuriates in her appetites, readily feeds extras who turn up, she shares your energy, your sparkling pleasure, but tries harder than you to understand those "who play at helpless," or the grim.
"Come back when you can smile," you said to me, but what would your response have been had you seen us as you died?

*

You gave, yet our wanting was not fostered – we were given to, not choosing, and choice could be an unfamiliar burden.
On first going to restaurants, deciding seemed something else to learn, an absolute to get right.

*

Like your sisters, you held up church fairs and school committees – cooperating to generate local institutions an essential part of being colonial – while he hurried home when he could.

You were the one with urges to get free of town, yet having accepted the order of things for wives and mothers, seemed to break us into that same mould.

Your standards were to be ours – with no dyed hair, or mutton dressed as lamb.

We, too, were to stand proud, head high, believing your advice was timeless.

Though I might vow your chant of manners would not be passed on, some of your ways have stuck.

*

You kept us round the family table (until your death flattened Christmas, birthdays and easy family meals). He was the quiet foil at the opposite end, his sedate ways and bland appetites teased by your rolling eyes and fiery tastes.

You were out in town, ready to captain each game played from School Governor to Women's Clubs but I later gathered from him that some nights you returned bruised and wanting his home comfort. He receded from a public place as soon as work was done, his views much harder to pin down and his tolerance wider.

By thirteen I'd began to say I'd do it differently from you. How that might be was far from visible, but declared intention was not to be a mother, "though I might adopt at fifty." I wasn't sure I wanted to be an adult if it meant giving up my nearest sister and going it alone, she'd always been ahead. She was the one who constructed the most optimistic version of every event, then accused me of imagination!

*

For you the necessary code for the instruction of young ladies was set – nothing personal.
Back straight, hair brushed and the using of a butter knife – rules requiring no amplification.
His concerns were more digestive – take small bites, calm down, then chew properly.
You seemed to eat anything, caution came from his more delicate constitution.

He got breakfast and in winter lit the fire before he got us going – up daughters – box the air, not each other - punch for life on icy mornings!
Even if he wanted gentler evenings without raised voices.

Although you had the high spirits, he apparently more sober, he preferred girls free to go, absconding being another colonial inheritance.
"You must leave", he said, "you can't just make your life with me because I'm now alone."

x.

Days circled round your easy ordering.
You set rules – not many – none excessive – and most made sense. Within them we played long hours in your dominion.
You held routines and we dined, danced or sang in your court.
You appeared to be the visible strength as we raced away to hills and bikes and friends.

It was unnerving if you were absent on returns, even if I dashed straight out again with the dog.
How could all that have seemed so certain solid?
Where it was precarious I failed to notice.

* *

You made substantial the control being a parent gave you.
His grew gentle. "I tried to set you the best example I could manage, not that you have followed." (The latter being far from true.)
He would be upset by bad behaviour, that was his weapon.
You set firm rules and put your substantial weight behind them.
We didn't get the chance to slice your authority off bit by bit.

*

Though rarely wilful or erratic, you demanded obedience.
You sounded fierce and felt responsible for maintaining high standards, but had no notion of meddling with how we made sense of things.
I used to say you expected to give us minds of our own and sex on our wedding day. Though I have always been grateful, given the power difference, that you didn't attempt to tell us what to think.

*

Your power and behaviour control were made obvious; as was our submission to demands that we not be caught fighting, not use bad language and behave decently as required. We still "act well" if family re-gather, so can appreciate you laid down clear expectations, yet the humiliations of your rule still linger.

As gentle shepherd he took us with him, no hectoring, no intimidation, he enticed us to behave with consideration.

You could be the barking sheep dog, with bite – asserting rights to control was of your time – we were yours to keep in order, with threats or force.

You had no hesitation in taking command, but cannot have been oblivious that demanding the submission of your daughters was complicated. Along with others you accepted once girls reached puberty they, unlike boys, should no longer submit to being hit.

And why did his decision fail to impinge on you?

Ahead of his time, he shrank from the common rule of corporal punishment, though disappointing him was misery.

If you struck in the name of the law, it was simple to hate you. And hate you again.

But when your death hit like nothing before, I couldn't decide what I thought.

He had drawn us into his belief in decency, as if it was sufficient.

With you dead that looked ridiculous.

While he, an agnostic, had another unsuccessful try at God, I ran back to the sea.

For years my curiosity focused not on your character, but on the lack of preparation for your death.
I'd rarely witnessed violence, except the force of school punishments and yours. And the first film I saw of war set me vomiting.

I fumed that you might have warned us there was a lack of foundation under any existence.
With you dead there was emptiness below the feet and in my belly pit.

Obviously I knew the fact of death but we aren't much attached to general facts.
The paper had one fact: you were the 165th to die on the road.

*

How could I not have seen you might suddenly die?
I had once wondered whether you might run away. If you were the tent pitched about our lives, he was the tent pegs. When we went on trips without him, there were uncertain dreams – with not enough to hold you, might you fly with the night wind?

*

Even our high and solitary mountain was not an absolute. Its bulk was there for us and even if cloud or rain obscured, the solid presence remained. Yet its myth told how, nursing unrequited love, it had stomped off from the three mountains inland. It was an extinct volcano that had erupted.

You were statuesque, a rock on sand.

I might kick at your ankles, while still seeing your motherhood as substantial.

I stayed believing in your dependability as you continued providing homemade sweets for every fête.

Of course, I could say that either of you might die, it's just that I never quite believed it.

With him it seemed nearly possible – he rolled a car once – sometimes work oppressed as worry – he could get "hot and bothered" – he didn't like my waking when I sensed he paced upset.

He felt fluid to move with, while you appeared to be a fixture.

*

Words were thin veneers rounding the hollowed shapes of "gone away", "not coming back" and "dead".

They are better placed in reverse order to reduce the grievance, but you'd gone back to where you once lived and were planning further travels.

Having wished to get away, you did so thoroughly, making it hard to accept that "you" might not have had any say in the matter.

*

Having taken for granted you were there to fall back on, suddenly you weren't.

I'd believed the difficulty ahead would be your firm hold. I half knew you could no longer envelope me, but you were the one to challenge if I wished to do things differently.

We might still be tied but I was on a long rope and you were to stand firm behind me.

*

You left me many questions, too much unasked and I soon began to over-probe a reluctant father.

Had you been there to hug and leave, keeping my letters as he did, would we have found our way through difficult conversations?

*

An aunt told me you wrote how much I tugged at your heart even if I "wouldn't believe that in a hundred years." Why not?

You also wrote that I didn't take the easy path.

But I have been grateful you seemed sure your children would be fine. You weren't an anxious mother and seemed bothered only when our brother was seriously ill.

Yet certain family narratives rolled on unquestioned – a version of me as too highly strung and not cuddling on your knee.

Whatever might have been problematic between us never got a look in until a favourite aunt filled me in – a perfect gift once I asked her for what seemed missing.

* * *

D

"Do not cut what you can untie."

Joubert

i.

Had you lived I doubt I'd have written of you. There is revenge in seizing you in words once you are unable to answer. After all you didn't claim full control of us, you kept your eye on our manners.

But you left puzzles, which proved to be recurring themes for my pen: after trying to take in that you really were dead, there was hurt from what you never said, but which I set out to disentangle. It is my difficulties that seek words and you vanished at mid-sentence.

*

How safe was it to love you?
Yet what else could I do?
Being newborn I just reached out and needed.

Somehow I gained a protective shell over my underbelly, long before your dying clinched the fact of it being risky to want you.

You were the one for me yet, as we all do, you had your difficulties.

*

A phrase of father's mother, who delighted her son found happiness with you and otherwise didn't criticise, would echo over years.

"How could you?" she cried at your chopping off my auburn curls. "You cut that girl back again and again!" And how I squirmed! This bursting forth was too alarming. I couldn't use an ally.

She spoke of what I wouldn't begin to face, since yours was the only game, at not quite five. A grandmother, with a different script, must be kept at bay, even though in waiting.

*

At what age did I wonder if I was too like father's side for your comfort?

You repeated just before you died that I should be confident in having character; though I didn't manage beauty.

His sisters liked the look of me but you didn't smile with pride as you often did at my lovely, blooming and flirting sister.

(While I with auburn hair pulled down as cover for the face, was waiting to fall for the man who gazed only to see my soul!)

ii.

It was being beside you that I learned to talk.
The offered building-blocks of words were hardly as
straight sided as you implied for whatever might be
between us.
Little wonder constructions of mine wobbled. Some
of my words, easily dismissed, were thoughts
floundering for a clarity you obscured.
With him shared smiles seemed sufficient.

*

I don't look at you and soften, as I do with his
photographs on my wall, reaching over the dead line
to tell him I'm tender or cross.

Communication faltered while you lived, as you noted
when you wrote to your sister, not to me, that I'd
never believe how far your heart strings were tugged
by my not making life easy.
You never spoke to me of this, didn't mention what
seemed unclear between us.
Through old photographs I search our history – you
hold me only in one small print of a christening at
four months.
Even in that you are busy.
Then we are together in a series of the family group,
shot not on aunt's Box Brownie, but by a
photographer, taken when I was three and still the
youngest.
You kneel and I pull away.
I stand and strain at an angle, not nestling as planned
into your straight backed, black haired beauty.

I can recall looking at you with pleasure while keeping my distance.

iii.

I know now you watched your father die of stomach cancer, yet anxiety was not health focused. Your own nearly always seemed robust and you were blasé about ours. A good night's sleep would cure us, you rarely troubled doctors.

You managed your life and ours with little fuss, only my brother had you running in concern.
Something in me sickened, watching that and wanting.
But of course my symptoms could be dismissed.
I blamed myself for getting it wrong, again, yet not quite knowing what was amiss, not being able to show I sought your care.
And not long after you left us all.

*

"Oh God, no!" you cried and fell to your knees in the hall outside my bedroom in that only moment of defeat I overheard. Father took the phone from you and was too crisp with gratitude. After you both disappeared into the night, a note left on the table, I was confused.
Had I imagined it, as a sister accused?
I couldn't be sure, although I'd heard your cry.
It took the headmistress at school next day to confirm I hadn't made things up, the awful had happened.

However, my brother made a recovery from his head injury, as you would not.

* * *

We were not accident prone before. A sprain here and there was as far as we went, except for a brother's jaundice and then this. Out of bed the note on the kitchen table read that we were to go to school as usual; out of bed dread in the dark was fading like a dream. Father re-appeared to shave. He could not have slept more than an hour before that call woke them and me. She got there first and groaned her "Oh no," while he went more slowly for a night call, then took the phone, his tone excessively polite and clipped to reveal distress "thank you... yes... thank you... all you can I'm sure... please pass on our gratitude."

They'd be angry I wasn't asleep; there had been other times I'd heard too much. I went to the window listening for the garage door, any sound might be some key.

By morning it was impossible to know what any of it meant. Their note implied any foolish fear would be another family joke and the ache in my chest quite possibly needed only deep breath. But I just could not sit still at school; finally it was "get out, stay in the corridor, you're nothing but distraction today." When I stood outside there came a bewildering torrent, yet I had no words for why I fell against the wall and wept. Was I once again to think only what I was told, or find some way to speak of the frightening? Soon the formidable headmistress bore down the long corridor, her head slightly to one side, and quite unbelievably she attacked the teacher and not me. Hadn't he heard? Well he should have, it had been announced in the staff room. Several masters were not in, they'd been up through the night on a rescue.

"Come my dear, tears won't help," she said and whisked me to the sick bay. Her deputy, with plaits tied round her more kindly head, brought me a drink, and I thought to confess that maybe nothing had happened, to say perhaps it was just my mistake. I didn't know what to believe but said I didn't get much sleep, and pulled bedding up as far as I dared, dreading to be caught as a fraud. She soothed a blanket "I know, dear." At the end of the day a sister was told to collect me. I didn't look near her eyes, but to my surprise she wasn't rough and as we biked she asked, "So you know?" The school had run with rumours I hadn't heard: "a head injury, it's definite." That certainty came from one whose father struggled with our brother on a stretcher. "They had to take his boots off, they weighed a ton." Our brother was proud of his boots, specially made for his big feet. One of the sixth formers carried the pair of them.

We were not asked to risk the mountain, to be burdened by boots down slippery scoria in the dark; we could best help by carrying on as if still asleep to whatever it was that had happened. Mother was busy going to hospital, she needed no fuss and no questions from us. Coping magnificently, people said of her, and she remained renowned as capable. Despite parental ideas of protection, I gathered satisfyingly gruesome detail to anchor what otherwise swelled unlimited. There were stories of tons of steel meant for a ski tow snapping to whip him round the head. "Now he will be loopy," one girl said. At home they decided "it's best the girls be kept away" yet later we saw for ourselves, on and off something black could still swirl him giddy.

iv.

Death and disaster might be handled with care, "not to threaten children," yet we lived in a land where our mountain claimed lives, conceivably the careless or disrespectful, but the distant volcano threw rocks as big as cars towards the virtuous as well. The earth quaked for all.

The fear I felt that all was not safe, the stories I told, kept most horrors down at the beach, away from us at home.

I understood the threat of undertows and whirlpools.

The sea rolled unceasing over black sand – swift rivers joined it along the coast and once drawn in could never re-form again – there was no way back to old shape from being one with the ocean.

But our home was protection, far more solid than castles of sand.

You said I had nothing to worry over, that you'd give me something to cry about, or told me to go to my room and only come out when I had a smile.

v.

Somewhere there was a "wrongness" in me not to be seen, or acknowledged.

If you hit me, might I be forgiven, not for the obvious broken rule, but for what went unspoken?

Did you ever see it mattered that, with a claim to total weariness, you'd turned away at my birth?

102

You, also, had been a "Daddy's girl" but was my attachment to mine annoying?
You handed me over, he said and I became the first baby he bathed and put to bed.

*

Your birthing of me was not difficult, but I was one too many, after a crisis with the baby before.
These were details I sought as an adult, when you had been fully broken.

There had been some question which couldn't be identified, apart from that brief panic as freckles appeared – a sign my unacceptable darkness was no longer hidden.

*

Camellias given to you and left in water those long weeks post birth, when "exhaustion" absorbed you, grew thin roots which took to earth and became that expanse of shining deep green leaf, blooming winter red, covering our garage.
It was known as my camellia and I, too, reached out for life from a start in water.
You told of the camellia and a thunderstorm bringing power lines down during labour, but not of your despair during the pregnancy, or that you turned away from us all when I was newborn.
Any of our complications were put down to faults in my nature.

While there was direct absorption, my flesh flourished and arrived full sized, yet once you had the power and choice shrinkage began, despite stirred cow's milk added at 5 weeks.

A good Plunket mother, you kept a record of crying, of my being un-obliging with fixed, required schedules.

vi.

Tenderness seemed not simple.

You asserted I was never a cuddly one, as if it must be my flaw.

I heard the blame and at three and a half watched the plump last baby stay comfortably on your lap.

But I still climbed on him, skin to skin, smelling his familiar head, playing with his chest hair, loving to touch his neck.

*

He was able to connect and comfort me.

He calmed baby me, and was the one to soothe the toddler, always attentive to the fact that a "highly strung daughter must unwind."

And he believed in his comforter role, we both did, holding to it long, long after its fault lines became exposed.

*

Contentment with him ended questioning. I did not wonder how there could be such peace that night, with him by the hedge, when the water tower lights came back on long after the war.

With you I began to believe the muddle belonged with the nature of your accident, the lack of help to grieve, or my being unforgiving of your departure. But maybe our knots existed all along. The peace there was with you came only in drowning out of life.

* * *

Was it shock which cut our connection? Father died eventually but threads never severed with him, he sank slowly and even had a trial run seven years before. The doctors made a textbook error and declared him about to die, so we all rushed back to be weeks around his bedside. Then he recovered. He took time and spoke of having loved; he did not crash out, dying without sending any message.

And you might have let me speak, not left me unused words. You could have said "despite our start..." you should have once acknowledged it. Years of disentangling made clear how it wasn't just the power lines which went down during your labour, you were felled as well. Friends, not you, told of despair over a further pregnancy, and you never spoke of those weeks after the thunderstorm. There can be no other beginning, that was what we had. Something was definitely too much for you. And was I just the final straw, not even the cause of it all? Your breakdown, "purely physical" as they hastened to say, took you right away. You did not stay in the local nursing home where physical collapses could be tended. Was your breaking not for scrutiny that you went far away?

You were the sun at the centre. During my growing years there was your shining, but clearly there must have been a time of eclipse. Once back in place you showed no hint of it. What awaited you in the dark? I had no idea. With him what pained was tangible, with you we only heard your scorn for weakness and your favoured maxim "when you want something done give it to a busy person," you being one. It was elsewhere I looked to ponder – to that neighbour pulled into darkness, who sank and sank until she was taken away – she showed the price paid when blackness got firm hold.

If we did recover from a bleak start, why could you never say? When you left, you left the unspeakable to me.

vii.

"Of course," he said. "Once you arrived we did come to love you" and for him no doubt it was a truth, but he was still there to acknowledge the unwantedness, he did not cave in as you did, temporarily at birth, and then, as I was leaving home, make it permanent. Twice was not easy to forgive.

*

viii.

The image which returns repeatedly is some fog between us.

I put stories there to reconstruct our history, as though these might explain, thinking that some missing fragment, which was never acknowledged while you lived, must be the crucial bit.

Yet usually the fog refuses to lift.

*

Old patterns between the two of us grew visible only slowly, to question my preferred belief in myself "as loving."

Once obvious, it seemed impossible not to notice your impact on me.

I had one set of lyrics which blasted too loudly through my days and nights, "If I am not wanted, I'll be off."

Being highly critical came readily to me, as you noted, while being criticised left me too easily defeated.

A bad combination you said – and were correct.

Since I feared to bleed and bleed from wounds of battle, and relied on his comfort, my sharpness lay masked while he lived, but the cut and thrust of fencing words are no longer hidden.

It wasn't that you also wanted me nicer than I was, you just expected the discipline of keeping thoughts to myself.

*

I tried to know more of you, not your lost body which I saw naked often.

Though words can't draw out the essential you I sought, these notes were a route of pitting myself against some puzzle.

It now seems likely that my enquiry was for what was not fully lived, not acknowledged, when we were side by side.

* *

My concerns could not be heard while they never found the right words.

It took time for me to see what was in question.

And there was a flood of relief that he could answer his half of it, even if he couldn't speak for you.

A beloved aunt offered her version; and your "friend", in anger with me, told what you would never have spoken.

All this made sense of that theme tune on repeat – for panic at "not being the wanted one" had slipped in beneath the skin.

*

I used to plummet down the plug-hole, en route to oblivion; whirling into sewers of "unwanted" there is no holding place to see proportion.

His insistence that only before birth, while a baby they already had might be dying, was I not desired, I knew to be true for him.

But he hadn't taken gin and a hot, hot bath.
He may not have known of the castor oil, though your friends did.

I was nosey you said yet curiosity is limited. And I am not quite sure what, growing up, I half knew but didn't question; though I also believed a sibling who told that my name came from "Barbarian", the outsider nobody wanted.

ix.

If criticised it too rapidly became an absolute – if guilt put a toe in it rushed me to that dead end of "not wanted". Once it flooded in there was no way to see weaknesses in perspective, any more than you could put yours in place. You just took a firm stand against them.
Your collapse at my birth was put firmly behind you, as if that collapse belonged to someone else.
You returned home, after two months, to cope with more than could pleasurably be managed.
An older sister, switched from a girl enjoyed to mini servant, felt you had moved from happy to irritated.
Yet over the years you talked boldly about keeping "delicate" for your next incarnation.

*

Offspring begin as part of us, maybe another start to heal ourselves, though we only call it "love".
Through them we expect to redeem the past.
Yet your pregnancy with me was an episode you had no wish to remember.

You spoke against the weak, as if you'd never been so vulnerable.

*

Perhaps my work with those who crack was also reparation for your subsiding.

As I look back over my stumbles through the unspoken, I see attempts to make sense, as well as the attention to human frailty you didn't like to acknowledge.

*

It came easily to tune into father's tension, yet it's not what I did with you and so assumed you'd just handed yours to God.

Perhaps you knew good health and life weren't up to you entirely, but I picked up only your confident assertions of strength, since your vitality graced my growing years.

*

You were the ground and I implanted, sending you to the end of your tether. Now I'm cut semi adrift from you as well as from our motherland.

You were what could not be encompassed – you were the earth for the seed of me. I grew within you.

To say "I grew" is a language muddle, for cells developed from no will of mine, long before there was any "I".

*

How had I confused the situation, curling round blame for an unfortunate conception?
Siblings might hold me responsible for the unpleasant housekeeper, her awful food and your drop into exhaustion, but what about you?
What was the residue of my arrival?

*

Possibly you assumed the past was best left unearthed, perhaps you couldn't believe it lingered as partial block in our daily engagement.
Certainly you didn't recognise I could only put a melodrama on repeat any time I believed myself "unwanted." You saw no need to give me details which, much later, helped to hold off devastation, allowing me to begin seeing the particular more clearly.

xi.

Back at our start, despite your intentions, I continued – out to survive and ruthless in taking all that was required. Your body was used.
Maybe something of this continued, if I recognised only your strength and power, assuming these to be fixed.
When my sister saw another aspect, I hardly wished to hear.
Did I not risk asking if you ever panicked that darkness might swamp you?

Could I not begin to look for your inevitable limits?
Nor did I enquire further when your friend, Ruth, told me in my teens, "You don't much like the look of me now, any more than you did at first! As a baby you were content with me as long as you never saw my face. So I developed strong arm muscles through keeping you at my shoulder."

*

How slowly, slowly my start with you unfolded.
You suffered too and must have felt lost, yet it was dismissed as only "physical depletion".
Siblings have their account of that grim phase, after my birth, while you went far from home.
But I can't go back from here to early incomprehension.

I was too young for words while we were both on cracking ice and I was not held with pride.
Yet at those times a fearfulness seemed to shadow me, you were infuriated.
Would all of this have mattered much to me if your next collapse had not been total?

* * *

E

We have as much right to complain about those who
teach us to know ourselves as that Athenian madman
who complained about the doctor for having cured
him of thinking he was rich.

La Rochefoucauld

i.

At 18 I went from the only home I'd known – could
go from those who'd shaped my days and years spent
beside them – never away for more than a rare week –
and be homesick, mainly for the dog.
A month later you were dead.
At 21 I took a ship across six weeks of sea.

*

There were reasons to leave but might I, also, fly away
from being the one whose arrival defeated you, one
tangled in hazy blame?
And might I escape the dead weight?
Being left and leaving became a theme.

ii.

In London I went to a medium who said you had "passed over" ten years before and my stream of tears should stop.

She didn't know they'd hardly started.

As father stood up from our huddle on the floor, we were to cope with it being public, then were exhorted to "carry on".

But how to also stay connected to our history and you? There lay the confusion.

Should we turn to stone for getting by?

Make a melodrama of living with death?

Just cut off, or grow indulgent with tears?

Between us siblings we tried all of these it seems. None of it much of a recipe to pass on, unlike those dubious books about "good deaths" or "good grieving" I later read, but the hotchpotch was what we could do.

*

I didn't care to be saturated by your death, after I'd just taken first steps out the door towards a city life.

Until the night at university we went to see off a friend – same group, same docks – where we'd waved to your ferry.

As I, later, lay on the floor one thing was certain, if I didn't go with it I'd be broken. The tumble of memory flooding in made clear, standing against it was no longer an option.

*

I must have been cross with you dying yet didn't
realise before the night I, who considered myself no
member of the church, decided to call on God,
beating my fury on a locked door.
Finding myself bolted out from consolation seemed
to be the point, for no attempt was made to go in by
day, when it would have been opened for me.

*

The lack of goodbye got stuck in a groove, as if a
proper farewell could have made it acceptable. I
wished to have had a better grasp of what it meant at
the time.
But what might that have changed?
Would the uncertainties between us have been
reduced?
Unnoticed I held onto "shoulds" - "it shouldn't be
like this," or "someone should have made it better."
Shoulds which kept me captive.
(Those who fight unacceptable deaths are much
admired, while the strength in submission goes barely
noted.)

iii.

That we can depend on ourselves and others less than
we hoped took slow comprehension.
We'd fed on belief that family would be there when
needed, as we, too, were trained for family duty.
We waited for your sister before the funeral. But she
dared not hug her nieces. She backed away from

where we sat to go and scrub the floor your friend
had washed already. (You had never been so
particular, one cleaning a week sufficient and we came
home to newspaper over it until it dried.)

This aunt who did not embrace our hurt said, "I knew
if I did I'd disgrace myself." And was still proud of
maintaining accepted standards over 30 years later.

*

A long ago constructed picture of family solidarity
unravelled, it grew clear that for each making sense of
your death it was a solo.

Instead of any sibling conversation I was left with this
self interrogation.

iv.

The jewellery that came from you somehow got lost,
and then the few remaining pieces went in a burglary.

I seemed unable to keep the valuable you left me.
Then my younger sister gave me one of your rings
and some days I put it on my finger.

And, one death anniversary, bought earrings to match
what was stolen.

At what point did I shape belief in riches gained by
your dying? It was held firmly for some long time, but
has dissolved somewhat.

Not those early and fleeting moments of prancing in
freedom from constraint. In later decades I was
grateful for an urgency not to postpone in case death
struck suddenly again. And it seemed to be a gift to
have been forced to see there must be uncertainty
beneath our feet.

*

Walking beneath a high and open sky it's possible to slide into feeling blessed for the parenting which once had been about me.

We were trained for gratitude – he made sure appreciation of your cooking was routine at meals. And if I found things to be grateful for in your death, it also felt lucky to have had your vitality alongside his more thoughtful ways.

*

For your August birth often I am away – a buoyant interlude of holiday from work and tax return or dirty floors, back to writing or feeling alive on an unexpected mountain path.

It reminds how you, too, sparked on trips.

But the birthday seems a minor event. It is your death day, on May 8th, and N.Z. Mother's Day in 1966, which left its deeper mark.

One year, for your birth, I am by the rough Atlantic, with no black sand, only the coarsest cream tossing in murky waves. Nearby I found the grave of another who, dying early, might not mind sharing his stone for a bouquet. Mauve flowers, as lavender was a colour you said I should wear, never pink, and there is tenderness as I lie flowers there to the sound of the surf.

v.

It was still possible, again and again, to feel stunned that you were never coming home to us.

I knew it as fact, and yet it could hit once more with sufficient strength to falter rhythmical breath.
"Whatever will be, will be," was one of your songs, yet years on I didn't seem to quite believe you could just vanish.

*

I tried to take on some of the provider role, after you dropped from office. And there was bravado in taking care of myself if you were not there to offer anything through the hardest moments of your death and funeral.
Had you lived we'd have had everyday frustrations and things to share. In the resounding gap I made a search through dried bones of mothering.

*

Any treasures gleaned from hunting over years, if laid flat, can be grabbed at a quick glance. I offer what has taken decades of accumulation to one who simply adds them to a long fixed, "a most complicated one, your mother," which is without curiosity in that complacency. I jump, with loyalty, to defend the best of you, their long dead in-law never met. I hear myself plump up the virtues, offering your sense of fun, capacity for pleasure and great efficiency. Even our coats were impeccably made.

* * *

Occasionally you are open to reclamation, then lie low again.

When a sibling complains at your having read foolish magazines not decent books, I hear myself agree.

Yet alongside your sister, on one N.Z. return, unruly longing for you starts to sprout.

And how she squirms as I speak of licking your cake cooking bowls, perched on the kitchen stool, simply being near your flesh and smell.

Where did those senses go as I coped without you?

vi.

Certain moments of contact come alive, yet I'd hoped to excavate a continuity.

We have lines of connection, yet I preferred to mine a seam making some passageway towards you. I couldn't quite accept there was nothing I could do to force you into an exchange.

*

Thirty years on from your death I want to tell you what I've done.

But would you have kept to notions of your own, assuming you already knew me?

You asked little while you lived and once when you did want to draw me in to your concerns, I wanted to get away, not realising that talking to you about anything would so soon be over.

*

That I was no longer open to your easy touch gave me a false illusion: pulling back provided no protection after all.

I wonder how I dared repeat the impossibilities in motherhood – offspring of our flesh and needing nurture, requiring to find their own way.
They might be kept in the heart yet push us back to take theirs elsewhere.
They go, to leave us birth torn again – and must take with them those fault lines of our loving.

*

Now, as sons who shared my days withdraw and attach elsewhere, I recollect a desultory edge, around what had been fuller for you, as we began our leaving, though then I rarely glanced at your dwindling satisfaction.
You died as your flirting prospects reduced and the menopause began.

*

While my sons grow wary, it makes sense that, of course, I felt the same with you in my teens.
I hear them finding fault, shrinking from excess affection and recall reluctance in case you were waiting to re-swallow me. And once I was turning to something new
did not want to be missing you, before you died or after.

*

You were no grandmother.
And my giving, which seems entwined with yours, continues... in reaching out to a new generation, I

120

wonder if you'd had enough of "warm hearted", of putting yourself aside for family duty?

Living longer than you means having to watch others begin what is now passed for me.

Having been central how easily would you have moved to the edges and born daughters starting all that lay finished behind you?

vii.

Though I thought of you reduced to pieces in that crash it was our expectations lying in bits.

And there was that intermittent rage over any illusion of completeness, at a body seemingly whole while we had to bear clarity in fragments.

What was lost was mothering and I learnt slowly to sink with grief, trusting that after night there would be day and after tears I might surface to joy over a flower in the garden, if it caught my eye.

One legacy, perhaps from our beginning as much as your end, is a sorrow in waiting. It can be a clean drop, bringing relief, holding it off is the drawn out burden.

*

Living absorbed me most of the time and these notes were sporadic.

Though events might also cut in to reopen tear flow: when an unknown boy dying in a London street was told by a stranger he had been loved.

And when I finally realised how far you put yourself aside for the girl in the ambulance as you had done for us - did you sing, as you often did, to keep our minds off horrors?

A friend's photo is left on the table after his mountain fall, for passing shocks that we would never see his face again. But no one picture captured mothering.

A card comes, recording someone else's cherished and grown daughter. Would you ever had made such a photo card of me to send lovingly to in-laws? I weep over it as I did decades before, visiting a neighbour's mother and finding the grandchildren framed in the sitting room, while you had not seen my babies.

* *

Only after it became admissible that life was not a whole I might ever gather in, was I returned to appreciating small sparks.

Sifting these old notes shows only difficulties were put on record.

Your gifts were simply lived.

Yet any scare brings you back, who so disliked the "morbid".

Being helpless over one son in New York, September 11, where a whole city witnesses the expected being shattered, throws me into something of 1966, which isn't usually there for recall.

Unable to do anything but miss you, miss him, I note, again, how solid innards can turn liquid, how panic is thrown out to any who might listen while it can't be digested.

Just as a collapsed lung of another takes me back towards that shocked disbelief I felt at your exit.

"The terrible is only story" – that is what we knew and hoped.
So my mouth opened and shut and opened and shut and opened too much, a ventriloquist dummy with no gut connection to dread.
A tale flopped from a clanked jaw, passed on in a vague wish for dissipation.

viii.

"How awful," some would say of your death, and I would think "how do they know, when what it has meant, even for siblings, remains uncertain?"
Yet these days I am simply touched by recognition that it was a decisive event.

*

A sadness settles solidly, after 34 years of absence, on this day of your birth – old, yet fresh as today's dew, and a grief to sit in – not a tipping hurt.
This longing for your touch, was hard to admit while it seemed you just quit, leaving us to manage.

* * *

Dreams still play out connection to your mothering and sudden departure.

Having woken from vertigo, it felt defeating if, contrary to expectations, sleep gave no relief from dizziness.

Once awake, a man I knew came to me with comfort in his tone – he could be rung any time, day or night, he said.

He was substantial, as though carved to emerge from rich rock.

And was the size a good father might be to his child.

Was he promising me security in his offered hand?

His presence was impressive and I quite certain he was there – that nearly monumental man.

Unable to find stillness I tossed and tossed. Yet must eventually have reeled into sleep.

By morning, with only traces of night nausea left, it was startling to see that man could not have been in my room.

I had dreamt myself awake and found him enlarged, with more substance, more opaque, than he usually is.

When I had sunk to sleep again there seemed no doubt that he had been present and I awake to hear him speak kindly in modulated voice, while he offered help in that gesture of his hand.

He was a decent man, though I couldn't quite trust in his offer.

I remembered another hand, no dream hand this.

A hand that was seen and often re-seen. It stretched out and over-reached – also offering more than could be given.

Two of us saw a young man climbing up, his sister following. Not that we knew they were siblings as we watched to speculate whether they might be a pair of lovers, each pitted against a high cliff face.

We sauntered in their direction with only casual interest. It was a chance to speak of our shared mother's death.

The day was sunny and we left five children playing behind us down the beach – mine small, her three heading into teens.

I was due to leave for London, and we might not get more time alone for several years.

We walked and watched the male reach the top, with its slight overhang.

The female close behind him.

She slipped a bit and shrieked; he, not hesitating, threw down his hand for her to take.

She reached at what couldn't take her weight. Had he lain flat with one or both arms hanging down from that overhang, she could have hauled herself up the final stretch. But he was crouching and reacted fast.

His fate was not as I'd, at times, imagined my own in a wilful act of throwing myself to make a point: "I'd show them!"

Display what exactly?

There lay some confusion. I registered only that if things were in pieces, why should I tolerate the seeming wholeness of my flesh, after mother's shattered in an accident?

While I half-believed she crashed out perversely, well, two could play at that!

I somehow believed I'd present a body broken into bits. Though that is not what the rocks did to the young man.

What I saw on the cliff face was entirely different. There was no volition.

He began as the one to the rescue. Immediately any place for will was wiped.

His body spiralled down, seeming to slow as it fell – a puppet suspended in the air with helpless, flailing limbs.

Once control of strings was cut he became an image of man without one jot of power.

He fell and fell and no act could make any difference.

As his plummet ended on the rocks, my sister threw up across my sandal. "We won't speak of this," she said, though perhaps we had just seen what I needed to know of mother's end, had witnessed again what was too hard to believe – that being subject can become an absolute.

We had children to get back to and left the limp body to three fishermen.

Presumably his sister waited on the ledge. She became irrelevant to that mesmerising fall.

With everything beyond him he could only dive right out of life.

The account in the news next day didn't speak of what we saw. It told that the saved girl was older than her only, now dead, sibling.

She cried out on that cliff and he instinctively took it on himself to offer her his hand.

*

A fall might become inevitable after clutching at what cannot hold us. If words are grasped against a rise of panic, how can they prove sufficient?

And the stone man's gesture was not quite to be believed. Perhaps he needed to see himself as caring and I would be awkwardly wrapped in some already framed picture of me.

Just as after mother's death I didn't want stroking, or potions for stress relief and sleep, but recognition of a different order.

"The Four Quartets", even if barely understood, was perhaps the greatest gift. A public reading of it threw only a little light but just enough to lift dread at too much confusion, at darkness closing down the day.

It set me in pursuit of clarity not comfort.

Too easy to claim "a quest for understanding" – a not quite reliable focus after parental care was relegated to the category of "false assurance."

If they regularly dropped us over the edge, we would, perhaps, have been better prepared, I began to say.

When the fall did come, abruptly, it left neither of them at their caring posts, for father too was drastically reduced.

If she cut off looking after us and did it on Mother's Day, obviously we'd cope! Of course it was possible if I braced myself. Though managing might mean hauling myself, shoulders first, not quite trusting a more relaxed body to do it.

Maybe I forgot the solace there could be in receiving, until Greek generosity from a good friend revived it.

ix.

Out to seek what might be driving me, I went through talking decades.

You, the one to kiss smaller wounds, or cook a healing soup, you who kept up routines, flung us into disorder.

I couldn't stamp or yell "how could she?" "She shouldn't just leave without goodbye?"
I wasn't three, still free to demand my own expectations of a mother - so, for as long as it took, failed to see the obvious that the only half acknowledged was still fuelling hurt.
You were the one to herd us, gathering to call our farewells and wave off friends or family.
That was the way we did things. You saw to that.
And then you didn't.

*

And while I ached for one "who understood," "who might have put it right," I failed to see there was no short cut to be given out by a "wiser" adult. There was only my own unsteady effort.
It took time before it occurred to me that dying might be a life time question, without slick solution, and where no one else's answer could do.

So what use these words can be for another ploughing through grief I can't know..

x.

You gave me life reluctantly and puzzles I assumed had answers, being too full of pseudo-mastery when you gave me sudden death.
Yet my search might not be wasted, if it was also towards acceptance of what eludes all capture.
If it began with hopes of finding, it became more toleration of how much must be in question.
Pages were written, bits and phrases, to gain small

control over what remains beyond my say – your death – my birth – the way it was to which I must submit.

Yielding to you was quite a different matter, and I'd had enough of that!

*

Gathering these notes written over decades, scraps in a folder, what shocked was the constant repeat of themes, just as certain childhood dreams lingered through years awake. One of which was of leaving to go alone.
Though I had no idea what might be out there, I seemed set early to lighten your grip, before you became the one to escape.

*

xi.

Your sudden severance left blood at the horizon.
Equally abrupt extinction remained the threat for us, for any we loved.

Getting old did not occur as a possibility for decades.

Though old age was definitely not for me, only sudden expiration, I didn't see the obvious that your end was fixing expectations, until Father showed a more predictable finish.

His staying through dignified decline became a precious gift. He gave a different kind of death, one which made sense.

What if I was to follow him?

How had I felt so sure I'd be like you in dying?

*

The absolute end of his smile and smell meant being left again.

But he did not flip up everything, or put his fatherhood in question.

He gave confirmation of a life all right and ready to be over which brought, along with tears, surges of gratitude that he stayed enough with us.

His dreaded death, as if it might bring a repeat of yours, did not sever me from him. Something stays comforting.

It suggests your dying was too disruptive of who I took myself to be – as if I'd had some protective shell from you, which shattered, leaving me apparently free but with a running yolk.

You were the containing shape, though fragile too, that much I'd failed to notice.

*

With him it never occurred to me to try and find all strands of fathering, he was not to be word chased.

You were gone and I wondered why I could not re-find a living connection as I played with your mothering skeleton.

* * *

Some things acquire a place and stay where they belong. My knives and forks in recent years remain rightfully slotted in their drawer, unless there's been an over eager guest. The dead too can be lain in order and engraved, though I failed to manage this with you. I did try, visiting your grave and then putting a photograph of it on my desk.

*

After he died, it was easy to distinguish the aged body that was gone from my history of him. Fierce crematory flames did not consume the father he had been. Though, once more, powerlessness was not willingly accepted. I had to be challenged before I knew that keeping love alive was not the same as keeping him. It took new life washed into darkness, rather than being brought to light, for me to let go of clutching at the ghost of him. Even here, where it was believable, for I'd recently spent six weeks with him and he said goodbye not once but twice, words did not carry full conviction until a miscarriage played out dramatically. Then it fell into place and I could weep at being left, at the inevitability of his death. He was missed

and he died as I would wish, like knife and fork this disparate pair lay side by side growing comfortable together.

A coffin arrives in the local church as I pass – an end
to a stranger's life – and it occurs to me it's taken
nearly forty years to put the shock of your departure
in place and better accept the inevitability of dying.
A task that took in many graveyards, absorbing how
everyone has their dead.
Yours stayed exceptional, until the graves of centuries
steadily softened the startling edge.

*

"Move on" may be the current mantra, yet with you
there have been inevitable returns: as I gave birth, at
your stopped age, which I matched and passed, and
through a long uncovering of detail around your
despair at my conception, with a collapse on my
arrival.
I was handed on to others then, and when you died I
did move on, yet kept walking into replaying cycles.

*

It is myself I had to forgive for that refusal to accept
it was as it was, and there was nothing to do but
suffer your death.
Instead there was occasional longing to see you just
once and, as menopausal symptoms hit, a flow of
sympathy, with questions.

xiii.

Your end left a thick wall – it seemed impenetrable –
as though you cut out and we couldn't hold out
anything more to each other.
Despite these efforts to seek you, are they just, brick
by brick, another disconnect?
There is no prospect of new life between us. For that
I thankfully have the living.

*

Blood thickens
with sad substance
that those once known
can then go,
and that your death blanked any exchanges in waiting.
For a sister-in-law recently showed what will never
now be shared, since her life by ending shapes the
finite.
It seems a simple and obvious fact she and I won't
have further conversations.
There was no such lucidity with you through those
early adult years. Years when the accidental in your
life and mine was not what I could stomach.

xiv.

I could say "one day we would all die," feel fear of the
sea as being beyond any safety of home, yet it took
your dying to hollow me, gradually, year on year, with
this as certainty.

The clutch of your mortality shaped me and, though not unrelentingly inhabited with conviction, sorrow over death itself became my companion.

*

It's not that I believe there will be no fresh and different thoughts about you but am flesh heavy with sureness that my own mortality is not just myth, and that interests me more than yours.
Yet this body burden seems shed by words flying light across a page, as once I tried to write myself free of that dead weight of you.

xv.

I have spun these story lines on sheets of paper, and find them true enough in the writing, in that quick move showing up the unseen, but what do they really net when put on repeat?
And do they play with "uncertainty" as a way not to fully accept where I am powerless?

*

I expected to track meaning, sure it answered, felt glad of ageing if, gradually, more seemed understood, until the balance altered. Somewhere late 40s, the meaningful, failing to accumulate sufficient, or lift sadness at what was past, proved less substantial after all.

*

If I supposed I might write you to life - a colourful kaleidoscope, where I heard your voice, felt your touch and sank into that smell - death was not to be overcome.

But words reached out towards something still between us.

And probing our history, through that slow digestion of what happened, holds on to being your daughter.

xxx

I sought to know you, but urges to make sense increasingly slip through a net necessarily woven with gaps.

If I thought once I might catch you and meaning, now it is being able to dance across a weave of holes, dance with nothing to hold, that is the delight.

*

Sedate like you I've never been and move still with tides and moon.

It may be hard recollecting flowing water, yet I have felt gathered, again and again, before a blank sheet where words etch brief clarity across much that stays filmy between us.

* * *

The End

Printed in Great Britain
by Amazon

KISS ALL YOUR THANK-YOU'S
GOODBYE

KISS ALL YOUR THANK-YOU'S
GOODBYE

RICHARD M. TIMBERLAKE

PALMETTO
PUBLISHING
Charleston, SC
www.PalmettoPublishing.com

Hardcover ISBN: 9798822951044
Paperback ISBN: 9798822957220